THE
SCIENCE
OF
MARKETING

THE

SCIENCE

OF

MARKETING

WHEN TO **TWEET**, WHAT TO **POST**,
HOW TO **BLOG**, AND OTHER
PROVEN STRATEGIES

DAN ZARRELLA

WILEY

Published by John Wiley & Sons, Inc., Hoboken, New Jersey.
Published simultaneously in Canada.

For general information about our other products and services, please contact our Customer Care Department within the United States at (800) 762-2974, outside the United States at (317) 572-3993 or fax (317) 572-4002.

Wiley publishes in a variety of print and electronic formats and by print-on-demand. Some material included with standard print versions of this book may not be included in e-books or in print-on-demand. If this book refers to media such as a CD or DVD that is not included in the version you purchased, you may download this material at http://booksupport.wiley.com. For more information about Wiley products, visit www.wiley.com.

Library of Congress Cataloging-in-Publication Data:

Zarrella, Dan.
    Science of Marketing: When to Tweet, What to Post, How to Blog, and Other Proven Strategies/Dan Zarrella.
        pages cm
    Includes index.
    ISBN: 978-1-118-13827-4 (cloth); ISBN: 978-1-118-26349-5(ebk);
    ISBN: 978-1-118-23306-1 (ebk); ISBN: 978-1-118-22528-8 (ebk)
        1. Internet marketing—Social aspects.   2. Social media.   I. Title.
    HF5415.1265.Z367   2013
    658.8'72—dc23   2013000733

Printed in the United States of America
10 9 8 7 6 5 4 3 2 1

To my fans, friends, and fellow scientists

Contents

Acknowledgments

THANK YOU!

All my fellow HubSpotters, especially Mike Volpe, Kipp Bodnar, and Rebecca Corliss. My lovely and talented wife Alison. My family Mom, Barb, BJ, Joe, Terri, Diana, Jenn, Gramma, and Grampa. All my friends from Wand Fight Team, especially Dave "The Pain Train" Mazany and Leandro Lorenco.

Introduction

I READ A lot of books about marketing. I read a lot of blog posts, attend a lot of conferences, and follow a lot of marketers on Twitter. I'm saddened by the overwhelming amount of superstition-based advice I see. I call it unicorns and rainbows—snake oil adages such as "Be awesome," "Engage in the conversation," and "Have a personality." These things sound great. And they're hard to disagree with; I'm not going to tell you to be not-awesome. But they're not based in anything more substantial than what sounds right.

And when we do get data about social media platforms, user behavior, or digital communications channels, much of it slowly emerges out of the scholastic system, produced by academics isolated from the marketing trenches. Science like this is interesting, sure, but it's largely data for data's sake, devoid of applicable lessons. We need more street-smart work conducted by researchers with real-world marketing experience. This kind of work is useful and efficient. It allows you to decide how to apply it so that you can do your job better.

As a social media scientist, I use data, experimentation, and real science to understand how people behave online and how we, as marketers, can leverage that behavior. I want to give you the data you need to get stuff done and to be successful.

1

But it is important to understand how to apply marketing science to your business. Think about the difference between how research works in fields such as physics and how it works in a field like medicine. In physics, there are mathematical formulas that show how a force like electromagnetism works. That force will always follow that formula.

Medical researchers, on the other hand, test new kinds of treatments on hundreds or thousands of subjects. From those experiments, they produce best practice courses of treatment. In specific cases your doctor will start with the most indicated course of treatment. If it works, great; you're cured. If it doesn't work, your doctor will try the next most indicated course. Best practices generated from large sample sets are tested in specific cases in which the results may differ.

It is this second example that teaches us how to use the marketing data in this book. My work is based on databases of thousands or millions of rows. My data span industries, audiences, time zones, and languages. I work to produce best practice suggestions from these data, but your business may be different. And I try to focus on data that aren't highly self-evident; I want to suggest new ways of doing marketing. I want to make you better at what you do, not just reaffirm what you're already doing.

The final chapter of this book isn't meant to be the end-all instruction manual on analytics. It's meant to provide you with a framework for applying the all the data I'm presenting, through the scientific method, to your business.

I work for HubSpot, a business-to-business (B2B) company that sells marketing software to a customer base that is largely using the Web to generate leads. My default mind-set when I approach marketing is as a B2B lead wrangler. Even so, often when I talk at conferences, I'm asked if the data I'm sharing can be applied outside of the business-to-consumer (B2C) world. Too many people think that "cool" marketing happens only in the consumer world and that B2B marketing has to be boring, stilted, and corporate.

In one survey I conducted, I asked takers if they had separate work and personal inboxes. A full 88 percent told me they did not. More people reported having a separate junk-only inbox. Focus group discussions have confirmed this as well. You'll read more about these stats in the chapter on e-mail marketing (Chapter 8), but the point is simple: business consumers are still consumers.

Boring is bad for B2C, and it's bad for B2B. Nobody wants to be put to sleep by marketing messages, regardless of what hat that person is wearing at the moment—personal or corporate. You need to be more concerned about being labeled "spam" than getting the right "work" e-mail address. If you're a B2B company, don't be afraid to make content like a B2C marketer. Be afraid to write white papers full of technical jargon like the rest of your industry.

I did the research presented in this book over a period of nearly five years. Throughout that time, I've noticed several threads running through the data. You'll hear about these concepts in many of the chapters to come, but I want to introduce you to them first.

The Conversation Doesn't Build Reach

One of the most pervasive bits of social media unicorns-and-rainbows advice I read is about the all-important conversation. The superstition tells us that if we're not constantly chatting with our Twitter followers, Facebook fans, or blog commenters, we're doing social wrong.

But when I looked around at the social media accounts that had the biggest reach, I was puzzled. Celebrities have a lot of Twitter followers and Facebook likes, but they don't do much chatting beyond their circle of actual friends. Media outlets are popular, too, but they just share a constant stream of stories. In fact, there aren't any good examples of people, brands, or businesses that are not celebrities, huge companies with giant advertising budgets, or extremely early adopters that have built large audiences in social through the so-called conversation.

In the chapters on Twitter, Facebook, blogging, and Pinterest, you'll see data that continually challenge the hegemony of the "engage in the conversation" adage.

Positivity Works Better Than Negativity, but Both Are Better Than Neutrality

Many times the data contradict the Kumbaya, feel good adages so prevalent in the communications world, but sometimes they don't. Sometimes they support it. Sentiment is one of those cases.

Typically when I've studied sentiment and its relationship to content performance or social media reach, I find that positivity does better than negativity. Your readers mostly don't want to get angry or sad; they want to be happy and feel good. We've all known someone who's a Debbie Downer or Negative Nancy. Even when we're sharing amazing news about our lives or telling a hilarious joke we just heard, these people have some bummer information to share to rain on the parade. After a while, you get sick of these guys and you don't want to be around them anymore. Don't be that guy.

The data dopes, however, hold an interesting twist on the old be positive saw. When I compared not just positivity to negativity but also both against neutrality, I found that neutrality performs the worst. It is better to be positive than negative, especially as a habit. But if you have a choice only between neutrality and negativity, negativity can work. Controversy and drama can stimulate attention and sharing, but tread carefully. Don't get a reputation for being a bummer.

Contra-Competitive Timing

Probably the most cited work I've done is about timing. Every time I release a body of research, some of the most popular numbers are the ones about time of day and day of week. So I've looked at timing everywhere I could, and in most of the places I looked, I found a simple, surprising pattern I call contra-competitive timing.

Imagine you're at a noisy party. People are talking, music is playing, and glasses are clinking. You're straining to hear what the person standing a few feet from you is saying. So you start telling a story, and about halfway through it, the entire party becomes silent for a brief moment and everyone hears about how you wet the bed until you were 13.

That's contra-competitive timing. It is easier to be heard when everyone else isn't talking. Too often marketers look for the time when channels are most active and assume that's the best time to engage. In my data about e-mail, Facebook, Twitter, and in some cases, blogging, I've found that weekends and evenings tend to have higher response rates than those times of the day traditionally considered busier.

During the business day, people have stuff to do. They're hard at work. Sure, they probably check Facebook or their inboxes, but they're pretty unlikely to be dawdling there for long. When they get home from the office, though, they've got more time. Fewer meetings and to-do list tasks are vying for their attention. And fewer marketers are sending e-mails and tweets. During which of these times do you think people are easier to reach?

In many of the following chapters, I'll cover the data that form the foundation of this theory. And I'll talk about how you can use these data to experiment with off-peak timing.

Social Calls to Action

Marketers have been using calls to action for centuries. We've known since the dawn of time that if you want someone to do something, the easiest way is to ask that person to do it. Online marketers aren't without this tactic either, calls to action (CTAs) such as "Click here," "Sign up now," and "Act fast" are all over the Web. But for some reason, when we started using social media for marketing, we lost all respect for the ask.

Irving Kirsch, a researcher at the University of Connecticut, did an experiment with a group of suggestible subjects (people who can be hypnotized). Half of the group was put under full hypnotic trance, handed a stack of 30 postcards, and had a hypnotic instruction implanted to mail one card per day back to the researchers. The other half of the group received similar stacks but were simply asked, not under trance, to send the cards back. The second group sent more back. When dealing with suggestible people, polite social requests work just as well as full on spiral-eyes trances and swinging pocket watches hypnotic commands.

Social CTAs work. They work on Twitter, on Facebook, and in blog posts. In upcoming chapters, I'll show you my research into which ones work the best and how you can begin experimenting with them.

Combined Relevance

A few years ago, I was doing some experimentation with an early social media site, Digg. I created a website, USBAbsintheSpoon .com and uploaded a Photoshopped image of an absinthe spoon with a USB connector on the end.

If you're not familiar with it, absinthe is a turn-of-the-century alcoholic drink that is supposedly hallucinogenic and definitely disgusting. It's very strong and is flavored with star anise. To make it more palatable, you have to add sugar, so absinthe spoons were invented: fancy slotted spoons that rest on the top of the glass. You put a sugar cube on the spoon and pour water over it into the absinthe.

My USBAbsintheSpoon didn't do anything. In fact, I never even made one; there was no spoon. But when I posted it to Digg, people went crazy for it. It got hundreds of comments, thousands of votes, and tens of thousands of visitors. In a few days, all the big gadget blogs on the Web were covering it and I was fielding calls from small town news reporters doing segments on the weirdest gadgets.

I had stumbled into a very useful tactic for creating social media content: combined relevance. When I took two seemingly distinct interests, absinthe and gadgets, and combined them, those people who were fans of both became super-fans of my spoon. It felt like it was specifically created for them. Turns out, however, that there are a lot of geeks who are also into terrible antique booze.

In the chapters of this book, you'll read suggestions for topics and words that perform well in various marketing channels. If your business operates in one of these areas, great; you've got it that much easier. But if your company is outside of those niches, you'll have to use combined relevance to get more creative. Think about how you can blend the subjects you're an expert in with those hot topics people love to read, forward, retweet, and like.

PART

I

Content

1

E-Books

As INBOUND MARKETERS, when we think of e-books, we tend to think of a content type closely resembling white papers: downloadable PDF offers designed to generate leads and sell our product or service. When the general population thinks of e-books, they're thinking of mainstream books in digital formats, typically on the Kindle or a tablet computer.

As the data I uncovered will show, there is a disconnect between entertainment-related reading in digital format and the acceptance of e-books for business-related reading. People are using e-books in large numbers, but not for business-related reading as much as we'd like.

To begin reaching the larger audience of potential readers who think about e-books in the latter way, we need to rethink how we produce, promote, and distribute our lead generation–focused e-books. This is the focus of this body of research. The class of web users who are already downloading your white paper–style e-books is already sold, but they're a small segment of your total market. I want to help you move into the scale of thinking like a mainstream publisher.

Survey respondents came from a statistically significant panel system and were not preselected for their preference for e-books of either the mainstream or lead generation varieties. In fact, while conducting this research I did a secondary survey using HubSpot readers and got vastly different results because they had already been sold on the idea of PDF-format business-related lead generation e-books.

The sample set consists of more than 1,000 American adults who own a computer or e-book reading device and have a job where they make $70,000 or more a year. The goal was to reach decision-making office worker types.

I asked survey takers how often they read e-books. In the first version of this question, I did not specify the type of e-book, because I wanted to gain an understanding of how people think about and interact with the format in general before exploring their use of business and lead generation–focused e-books.

Approximately 65 percent of survey takers told me that they read e-books at least once a month, with a quarter reporting that they read them more than once a week (Figure 1.1).

Clearly, e-book use is becoming a mainstream phenomenon; popular reader hardware has been available for only a couple of years, and already, most of the popular books are consumed as digital content.

Although Figure 1.2 gave me hope about the level of e-book adoption in the general population, the business book–focused version of the question painted a somewhat more challenging picture.

Just less than half of the survey takers said they read business-related books ever, with less than 10 percent reading them more than once a week.

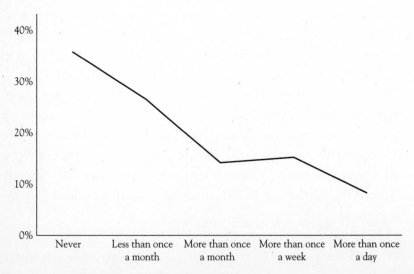

Figure 1.1   How Often Do You Read E-Books?

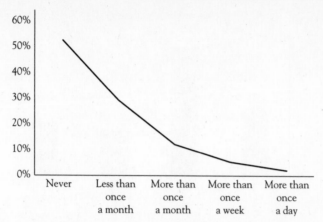

Figure 1.2   How Often Do You Read E-Books for Business?

Comparing this result with that of the generalized version of the question demonstrates that there is a large opportunity for lead generation e-book producers to reach readers who are already consuming digital book content and get them to begin reading business-related content.

Diving deeper into the issue of business-related e-book consumption, I asked survey takers what categories of e-books they read.

The most popular format, with nearly half of respondents reporting, was fiction e-books (Figure 1.3). Consumers are shifting their nondigital reading habits to electronic formats and reading best-selling books such as *Hunger Games* and *Twilight*. As I noted earlier, this tells us that the challenge isn't so much to sell readers on the idea and format of digital books but to persuade them to do their business reading in a format they're already comfortable with.

As e-book producers, we need to study the promotional and production techniques of more traditional fiction publishers and apply them to our lead generation–focused content.

In the survey, I asked the takers to indicate their gender, so I was able to break down responses into men and women; I've highlighted that division where there were interesting differences. In this instance I found that men seem to have a higher likelihood than women of reading business-related books in digital formats (Figure 1.4).

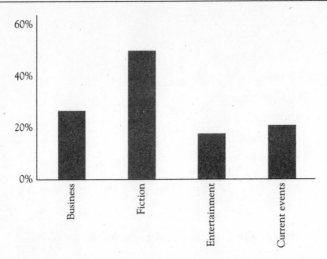

Figure 1.3   What Kinds of E-Books Do You Read?

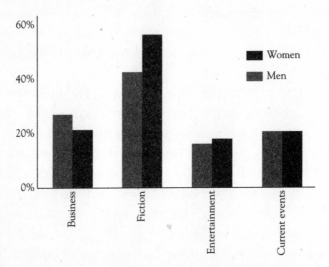

Figure 1.4   What Kinds of E-Books Do You Read? (Based on Gender)

This tells us that if we know our audiences well and we know that they skew to one gender or the other, we need to be aware of their preferences and promote and sell our content accordingly. In female-heavy markets, more time and effort must be spent on persuading readers to use electronic formats.

I also asked respondents how they hear about the e-books they read. Their responses demonstrated the market leadership that

Amazon and its Kindle format commands in the e-book world. Approximately 45 percent of survey takers reported that they find out about new e-books directly from Amazon (Figure 1.5). This is a powerful argument for getting your digital content onto Amazon.com and in the Kindle format.

The second most common response was recommendations from friends, underscoring the importance of word-of-mouth marketing in the e-book space. Be sure to explain to readers, both on e-book landing pages and inside the books themselves, how they can share the book with their friends.

The third most common way that readers hear about e-books is through search engines. Your landing pages must be search engine optimized and show up in searches for relevant keywords.

When I split respondents into gender buckets and analyzed their answers, I found that men report finding e-book content through search engine queries more often than women do, whereas women are more likely to find new books directly through Amazon (Figure 1.6).

This is helpful to know, because it can help you prioritize your promotional efforts. If your market or target audience is heavily

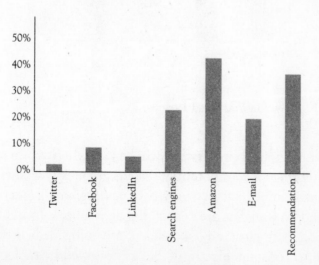

Figure 1.5   Where Do You Hear about E-Books?

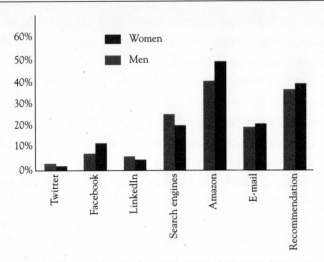

Figure 1.6   **Where Do You Hear about E-Books? (Based on Gender)**

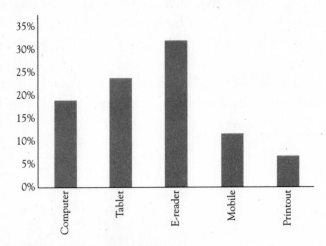

Figure 1.7   How Do You Read E-Books?

male, search engine optimization will be key, whereas Amazon may take center stage if your potential readers are mostly women.

E-books can be read on a variety of devices, so it is important to understand how readers are consuming digital book content.

I found that most e-book readers are using dedicated reader hardware to consume electronic books, followed by tablet devices and desktop computers (Figure 1.7). This ordering of preference differs from the way most lead generation–focused e-book producers think about their offers, but to readers, e-books are all e-books.

As marketers, it behooves us to ensure that our content can be read on whatever devices our readers wish to read it on. We should be making the experience of consuming our content as pleasurable and seamless as we can, not imposing artificial restrictions, such as using formats and delivery systems that mean our e-books can be read only on desktop computers.

Again, we find an interesting difference between men and women on this measure. Women are more likely to be reading e-books on dedicated reader hardware than men are. Men, on the other hand, use tablets and computers more than women do (Figure 1.8).

This information should also be used to prioritize our efforts. If your market is female-driven, you need to be sure that your e-books are available and optimized for reading on e-reader hardware. This may mean providing your books in Kindle format.

Digging into e-book formats, I found again that Amazon's Kindle format is the clear leader in the electronic book space, with the PDF format trailing in second (Figure 1.9).

This highlights the importance of experimenting with releasing your e-book content in the Kindle format. Several services exist that can help you manage this process, and the data clearly indicate that you should take advantage of this.

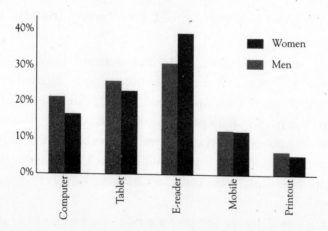

Figure 1.8   How Do You Read E-Books? (Based on Gender)

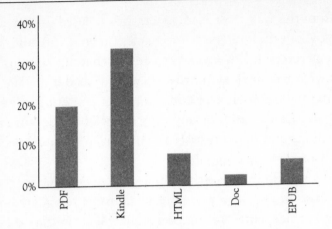

Figure 1.9   What Is Your Preferred E-Book Format?

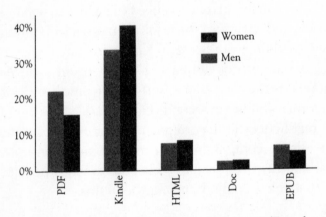

Figure 1.10   What Is Your Preferred E-Book Format? (Based on Gender)

The gender breakdown reiterates a trend that should now be becoming obvious. Women are more closely aligned with the Kindle system than men are (Figure 1.10). And the evidence is piling up that if your audience is women-led, you need to seriously think about how to get your content into their preferred format and their chosen device. If your audience is largely men, you may have more breathing room as far as sticking to the PDF format is concerned.

Asking how long readers prefer e-books to be provided an interesting insight. Respondents appeared to prefer either very long or

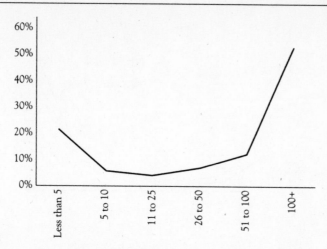

Figure 1.11 How Many Pages Do You Want E-Books to Be?

very short e-books, but they had remarkably little interest in e-books in the middle (Figure 1.11).

Readers likely think of very short e-books as quick, easy reads and are not concerned about wasting their time with them if they're not worthwhile because they'll be able to read them in an hour or less. Longer e-books, on the other hand, are probably seen as more valuable and substantial resources—as "real" books.

Your decision to write one length or the other should be based on your business goals. If you want a high volume of leads and are less concerned with the quality and commitment of those leads, shorter e-books are the way to go. But if you'd like to attract more dedicated readers, albeit fewer of them, experiment with books 100-plus pages long.

The men versus women breakdown of these data shows us that women seem to have a higher preference for longer e-books than men do (Figure 1.12). Again, use this information to inform your experimentation with different e-book types based on your knowledge of your market, target audience, and potential readership. Create shorter books for male-dominated segments and longer ones for female-dominated segments.

When I directly asked readers if they preferred physical, printed books or e-books for business-related reading, the results were

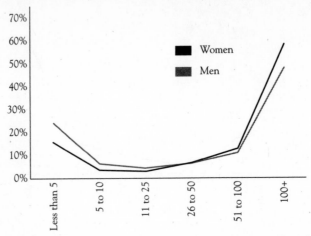

Figure 1.12   How Many Pages Do You Want E-Books to Be? (Based on Gender)

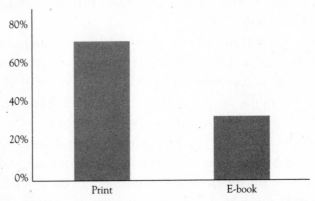

Figure 1.13   Do You Prefer E-Books or Printed Books for Business-Related Reading?

somewhat disheartening. Close to 70 percent report preferring printed books (Figure 1.13). Although I'm not sure why this is true, given the acceptance of the e-book format for fiction reading, it does present a significant challenge.

Not only must your landing page and promotional material sell readers on the content of the e-book itself, but if you wish to reach an audience larger than those who already regularly read business e-books, you'll need to persuade readers that digital books are worthwhile.

What Do You Like about E-Books?

- **Convenience.** The vast majority of positive feedback given by survey respondents centered around how convenient e-readers and e-books are. Responses typically referred to two elements of convenience: size and immediacy.

  Because e-books occupy only virtual space, a user can store a large number of them in the same amount of space that would be taken up by a single small physical book. Respondents reported enjoying this quality because it freed up shelf space in the home and made their book collection mobile. They can now easily travel with hundreds or thousands of books in their pocket or bag.

  E-book readers also note that they value the immediacy of acquiring a new book. If they find out about something they want to read while browsing the web or through a recommendation from a friend, they can instantly download it. They can get new books in a matter of seconds both from their desktops and from mobile devices.

  When producing e-books for marketing purposes, we need to move beyond thinking about them as simply PDF downloads that readers will consume while sitting at their desks in their offices. Users want to consume content while on the go, and their two biggest reasons for preferring e-books center around untethered access. Think about, optimize, and promote mobile use of your e-book content.

- **Price.** Although users were split on the issue of e-book pricing, many listed it as a positive feature of the format. Survey respondents were pleased that e-books are typically less expensive than their physical counterparts. This serves to reduce the risk of buying one. If they don't like it, they've wasted less money than they would have if they had purchased a hardcover or paperback.

  Most marketing-focused e-books being used for lead generation are free, and as marketers, we can sometimes forget that a price of zero is a potent selling point. In most areas of their life, our target audiences pay for content they want, so a free book is a good deal. Do not hesitate or forget to include this in your marketing copy.

- **Changeable Font Size.** Many respondents indicated that they were thankful for the customizability of the font and font sizing of text in e-books. Older readers can have trouble with small print, and e-books provide an easy remedy for this by allowing them to simply make the text bigger.
- **Ecological.** Because they're not made of trees and produce no waste material that must be thrown away, readers believe e-books to be more ecologically friendly. This echoes the sentiment that can be seen in many e-mail signatures along the lines of, "Think before you print this e-mail out; save a tree."

  Green is a timely and powerful value addition to marketing efforts for a variety of products, and it can be added to the copy on the landing page for your e-book. Remind potential leads that e-books help save trees and reduce landfill waste. Readers of your e-book will be doing their part to keep the Earth healthy.

What do you dislike about e-books?

- **Tactile Deficiency.** The most common problems respondents listed about e-books were related to tactile issues. The most common phrase used was that electronic books were "just not the same." Many people reported that they missed the sensation of flipping pages and the smell of physical books. Others simply said that they did not like that they were "not paper." Many of the respondents who voiced issues like this had difficulty expressing exactly what they found disconcerting about the lack of traditional tactile qualities.

  I believe this problem is merely one of time. As e-books and e-readers become more ubiquitous, users will begin to form the same kind of positive associations they have with traditional books. Until then, an interesting tactic is to commiserate with the potentially weary reader about how e-books "don't smell the same" in a humorous manner, addressing their concerns and helping them identify with you as the author.
- **Price and Equipment.** Many respondents discussed the issue of e-book pricing in two parts: the initial cost of the equipment

required to read them and the fact that in some cases e-books are not as much cheaper than physical books than they would like them to be.

E-books can, of course, be read on a variety of devices, not just dedicated reader hardware such as the Amazon Kindle. Although there are great benefits to these kinds of devices, readers are not limited in their access to electronic books merely because they don't have a Kindle. Remind readers that they can read your digital books on any device or platform they want, including desktop and laptop computers.

Again, in the context of lead generation e-books, most of them are free, so do your best to highlight this fact when "selling" your content to your readers.

- **Eye Problems.** Some respondents lamented sight problems with reader hardware. They report that reading on screens hurts their eyes. This is a hardware problem, and not much can be done to alleviate this issue by the producer of an e-book other than to remind readers that they can consume the book on any device or screen.

- **Sharing.** Survey takers reported that they disliked being unable to share digital books in the same way they can share physical books. They note that lending a traditional book to someone is as easy as giving it to that person.

This, of course, is merely a misunderstanding of the technology of e-books. Depending on the format, sharing e-books is markedly easier than sharing physical books. In the case of lead generation–focused, free, PDF e-books, sharing isn't even the correct way to think about giving the book to other people. When you give a traditional book to a friend, you no longer have a copy of it for yourself. On the other hand, with digital books you can simply direct a friend or coworker to the landing page for an e-book and he or she can also have a copy.

In the case of Kindle-formatted e-books, sharing features do exist. Once readers understand them, they can share e-books across great geographic divides, something that is more difficult with physical books.

Include calls to action and instructions on how to share your e-book both in the landing page copy and inside the book itself.

- **Screen Time.** Some respondents said that they spend all day working in front of a computer so they value their after-hours reading time as time spent away from screens. This is a difficult objection to address other than to perhaps remind readers that they can print out your digital content and read it on paper, although this may be a viable option only if your content is reasonably short.

- **Nonwaterproof.** Many people report that they read books in either a pool or bathtub and explain that they don't like the fact that e-book readers are not waterproof. Although this is somewhat confusing because paper books can, in fact, be easily damaged by water, it is fairly easy to address. Several models of tablet computers (which can be used as e-readers) are waterproof. If you think your readership reads in the water a lot, this is an option that may be useful to remind them of.

2

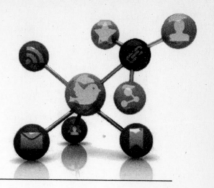

Webinars

My FAVORITE KIND of content to produce is webinars. I love speaking, live, in front of a group of people, both physically present and virtually. And webinars present a unique ability to scale to sizes not possible at real-life conferences. In fact, I hold the Guinness World Record for the world largest webinar—we had 30,000 registrants and 10,890 attendees.

I spend a lot of time working to improve my presentation skills, and part of that time was spent studying webinars and presentations from a scientific point of view. I did qualitative research, with a survey and expert interviews, as well as quantitative measurement of actual tweets about a big webinar we did.

I started with a survey in which I asked takers, through an open-ended paragraph entry field, "What makes you want to tweet or blog about a presentation?" I read through the thousands of responses, by hand, and grouped them into a handful of different topical categories.

In Figure 2.1 you can see the most common reasons survey respondents gave. "Sharing" answers told me about a desire to share what they were hearing with the world around them. "Novelty" and "news" answers said they tweeted or blogged news and newsworthy information they heard. The "relevance" answers indicated that they thought about how the information they were hearing would interest their Twitter followers or blog readers. "People there" answers reflected that they were thinking about the community created by other people in the audience of the webinar they were

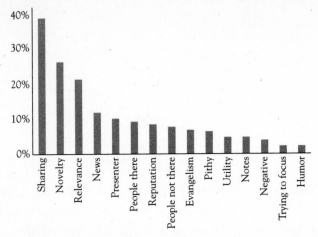

Figure 2.1   What Makes You Want to Tweet or Blog about a Presentation?

attending, and the "people not there" answers specifically wanted to share the content with people who could not attend.

Another way in which I studied webinars was to analyze the timeline of a popular webinar we presented at HubSpot: The Science of Facebook (Figure 2.2). I gathered all the tweets using the #FBSci hashtag (seen in the thicker, darker line) and plotted them against the webinar platform log-ins (seen in the thinner, lighter line).

What was interesting about this webinar example was the log-in time. We were scheduled to begin at 1 PM, but we had so many people log in that the software crashed and attendees were unable to gain access for about 20 minutes. Notice that the volume of tweeting did not decline during this period; if anything, it increased.

Many of the tweets that were sent during the technical difficulties were complaining about not being able to log in, but the hashtag trended earlier than it would have otherwise. And once we were able to get going, the feedback was overwhelmingly positive. As long as you're communicating with your attendees and you do eventually manage to provide value, you don't need to worry too much about technical glitches.

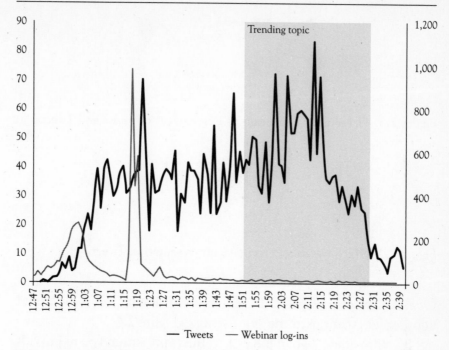

Figure 2.2   Presentation Activity over Time

In that same webinar I used a tactic I call takeaway slides. These were simple slides placed throughout the presentation that contained neatly encapsulated 140-character or less explanations of what the audience had just heard. Each slide contained a Twitter icon and a mention of the webinar's hashtag in an attempt to encourage tweeting of those takeaways.

When I analyzed the tweets from the webinar after the fact, I found that although 22 percent of the slides I presented were these takeaway slides, less than 9 percent of the tweets used the text from them (Figure 2.3). I still use takeaway slides in many of my presentations, but as a result of these data, I no longer rely on them to stimulate a bulk of the social media sharing.

Although takeaway slides didn't produce the volume of tweets that I had hoped for or expected, I did notice that a very significant portion of the webinar's tweets were actually retweets (RTs).

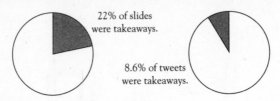

Figure 2.3   Tweetable Takeaways as Percentages of Slides and Tweets

Figure 2.4   Retweets as a Percentage of Presentation Tweets

Of these tweets, 27 percent used the traditional "RT" syntax and another 5 percent used the "via" syntax (Figure 2.4).

If you're doing a good job as a webinar presenter, you're providing much value to attendees in an entertaining, engaging way. This means that they probably don't have a ton of time to switch over to a Twitter client, compose an original tweet about your content, and post it. Many of them will save time by retweeting what other attendees are saying.

As a result of these data, I began experimenting with PowerPoint plug-ins that allow me, as the presenter, to write a set of tweets and attach them to specific slides. When I advance to those slides during the webinar, the software automatically tweets through my account. At the start of the webinar, I tell attendees that I'm doing this and that they can simply follow my account and retweet what they like.

During many of my presentations, I do social experiments that involve asking audience members to raise their hands in response to a set of questions. Typically, I'm doing this at a live, in-person presentation. I've also begun doing it during virtual presentations. I specifically ask attendees, in their offices, alone at their desks to physically raise their hands in response to my questions. And during the Facebook Science webinar, I took it a step further and asked them to tweet at me that they had, in fact, raised their hands.

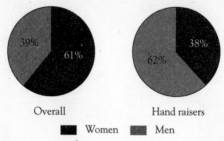

Overall Hand raisers

■ Women ■ Men

Figure 2.5 Hand Raising and Gender

When I went back through the presentation's tweets, I found that although my overall audience breakdown skewed 61 percent female, the users who reported complying with my hand raising request were 62 percent male (Figure 2.5). As is often the case with gender-based breakdowns, I don't have a great reason for this phenomenon, but the best suggestion I've heard is that male listeners were more convinced by listening to another male give them a request.

For marketers this is just another reminder that it pays to know your audience. Do demographics research; find out if whether your audience skews male or female, what ages they are, what they do for work. And don't be afraid to conduct surveys to ask deeper, more qualitative questions like what they want to hear during your webinars.

I then categorized the users who tweeted about my webinar into the three groups mentioned in the previous graphs—hand raisers, takeaway sharers, and retweeters—and analyzed the average number of followers each group had (Figure 2.6). I found that those users who retweeted content had more followers, on average, than the other groups and the overall average.

This means that your most influential and high-reach attendees might be the most likely to be too busy to write their own tweets. These are the users you'll be reaching when you use automatic tweeting plug-ins, so it's worthwhile to at least experiment with them.

After most of our webinars at HubSpot, we upload the slides to presentation-sharing site SlideShare. I gathered data on tens of thousands of presentations on SlideShare and compared the

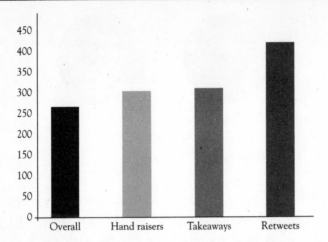

Figure 2.6   Median Number of Followers by Tweet Types

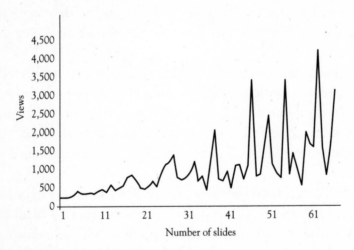

Figure 2.7   SlideShare Views by Slide Count

number of slides each was composed of to the number of views they had received (Figure 2.7).

I found that as the length (in slide count) of a presentation increased, the number of times they were viewed also increased. These data suggest that people on SlideShare prefer long, information-dense, comprehensive presentations.

As a general rule of thumb for presentation design, I don't use bullet points and I keep my slides to a single point. This means that I typically have just less than one slide per minute of live presentation. Most of my presentations are 60 to 90 slides. This is good practice presentation design, and the data here show it's also useful for slide-sharing sites.

PART

II

Channels

3

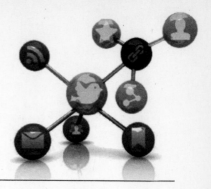

SEO

My FIRST INTRODUCTION to the practice of online marketing was through search engine optimization (SEO). I began my career as a SEO expert and did that for five years. It taught me the fundamental nature, and, more important, the feasibility, of return-on-investment (ROI) tracking and the get-stuff-done attitude that doesn't wait for big-budget allocations to make things happen.

I learned about how the Web would change marketing from pushing, intrusive, interruptive, outbound practice to a user-driven, pulling, inbound process. I studied keyword lists to discern user intent and pored over analytics reports to ensure websites were filling user demands. I learned a lot from working in SEO; I owe my career to it.

Over the past few years, I've come to realize that SEO as a distinct discipline is outdated. What we used to call link baiting is now simply the creation and promotion of good content that will naturally draw traffic and links. On-page optimization that used to be keyword density analysis and header tag tweaking has largely been outsmarted by the piles and piles of genius brains working at search engine companies. And spider friendliness issues have been all but entirely solved by modern content management systems— at least those worth paying for. Given my roots in SEO, I didn't arrive at this conclusion lightly. I have friends who still work in this field.

This chapter is composed of my research into the topology of the modern SEO field. The most important takeaway you should leave this chapter with is that you probably don't need more SEO help. Most businesses would benefit much more from increasing content quantity and quality.

When I started studying SEO, I wanted to approach it from a fresh angle. There is a lot of quantitative research out there about SEO analyzing it from the perspective of the search engine spiders and algorithms, but I wanted to approach it from the user's perspective so I started with a survey.

The first question I asked my survey respondents was multiple choice: "Where do you find information online to support purchasing decisions?" Somewhat unsurprisingly (at least to experienced digital marketers), the top answer was search engines, followed by social media and blogs (Figure 3.1).

Even in this age of Twitter, Facebook, Tumblr, and Pinterest, search engines remain the primary source for research for customers close to buying a service or product. Don't chase the newest, shiniest social platforms all the time and forget about the basics. Search traffic is still important.

Then I asked my survey takers, "How often do you make purchasing decisions based on information found through web searches?" I

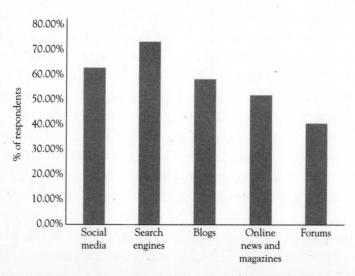

Figure 3.1   Where Do You Find Information Online to Support Purchasing Decisions?

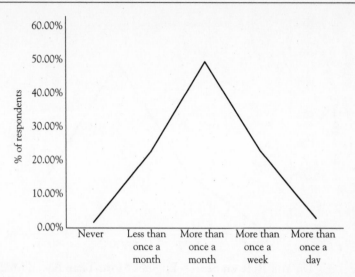

Figure 3.2 How Often Do You Make Purchasing Decisions Based on Information Found through Web Searches?

found that the most common answer—just more than half—was "more than once a month" (Figure 3.2). The rest of the responses were distributed, bell curve–style, around that as a median.

This means that not only are search engines the most used source of information for purchasing decisions, but they're also consulted, by more than half of my respondents, a least once a month. If you weren't already convinced that search traffic was key to your business, you should be getting the picture now.

To drive home the point about the perceived importance of social media versus search engines for buyers online, I directly asked survey takers, "Do you rely on search engines more than social media for purchasing decision information?"

Sixty percent of them told me they rely on search engines more than social media "frequently," and about 20 percent said that they "always" rely on search engines more than social media (Figure 3.3). Only 20 percent answered "rarely" or "never." It is indeed a rare Web user who uses social media solely when deciding to buy something. The vast majority of them (around 80 percent, in fact) typically rely on search engine information more than social.

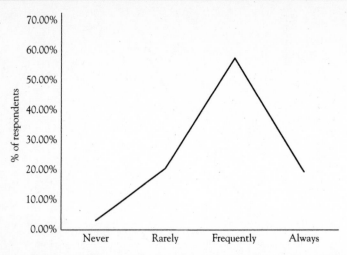

Figure 3.3   Do You Rely on Search Engines More Than Social Media for Purchasing Decision Information?

But we shouldn't take the last few graphs to mean that social media is useless compared with search engines when we're trying to sell something. To the contrary, in fact; social media can be used to augment our search engine marketing efforts.

Using SEOmoz's great Linkscape database, I analyzed thousands of links across the Web and compared the number of times they were tweeted and the number of incoming links they had pointing to them. I found a positive relationship; that is, as the number of times a link was tweeted increased, so did the number of links pointing at that URL (Figure 3.4).

This is not to say that simply tweeting a URL gets it links; rather, tweeting a link can help it get in front of the right kind of Web users. Rand Fishkin calls the special class of people who have the power to create a link the linkerati—typically folks such as bloggers, journalists, and savvy social media users. And many of these linkerati are on Twitter when they're looking for content to link to. Be sure your pages are there, too.

I also looked at the relationship between the number of times a page is shared on Facebook and the number of incoming links that page had pointing at it, and I found a similar positive relationship

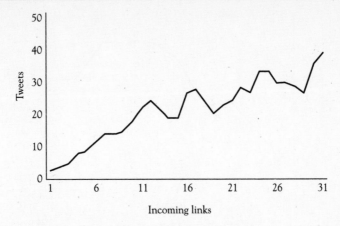

Figure 3.4   Relationship between Tweets and Links

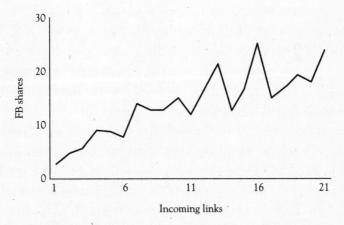

Figure 3.5   Relationship between Facebook Shares and Links

(Figure 3.5). As the number of Facebook shares a URL has increases, the number of links it has also typically increases. Facebook, too, can be used to enhance our SEO efforts.

The final specific social media platform I investigated with the SEOmoz data was LinkedIn. And as you might guess, here I also found the same positive relationship between sharing and linking (Figure 3.6).

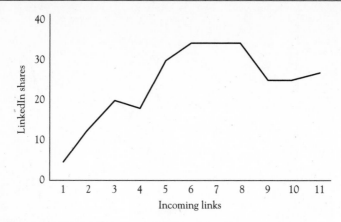

Figure 3.6   Relationship between LinkedIn Shares and Links

The average number of LinkedIn shares was much lower than the average number of Facebook shares or tweets for the URLs in my data set. This is because LinkedIn isn't as popular of a content sharing network as the other two. For a marketer this represents an opportunity. There may be less competition for interesting content in your industry on LinkedIn, so don't neglect it.

Once I noticed that all three of the major social media platforms had positive relationships between content sharing and incoming links, I wanted to compare them in a meaningful way for marketers.

I analyzed them using a metric called Pearson's coefficient of correlation. This number represents the strength of a relationship between two numbers. If it is above zero, the relationship is positive, as is the case for these data (Figure 3.7). A perfect positive correlation (such as age and birthday) is represented as 1. Most correlation relationships are less than 1. For instance, SAT scores are typically correlated with college grade point average by a coefficient between 0.2 and 0.4.

What I found was that although all three social platforms had positive, significant relationships, the strongest was LinkedIn, with a score above 0.5. This means that LinkedIn is a very important network for marketers to experiment with when they're sharing content in the hopes of attracting links.

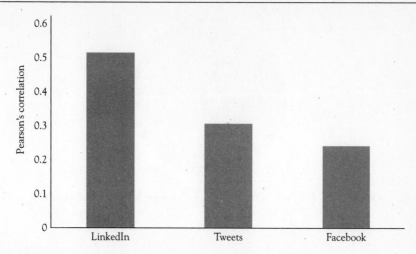

Figure 3.7   Correlation between Social Shares and Links

Figure 3.8   Do You Believe That Web Pages Ranked Higher in Search Results Are More Trustworthy Than Those Ranked Lower?

Going back to the survey data, I asked respondents, "Do you believe that web pages ranked higher in search results are more trustworthy than those ranked lower?" What I found, although not entirely unexpected, is somewhat concerning (Figure 3.8).

Slightly more than half of my respondents said "yes." Think about that for a second. More than half of the people who come across your site in search engines may believe that the sites positioned above yours are more trustworthy. If you've been around digital marketing for any length of time and understand what it

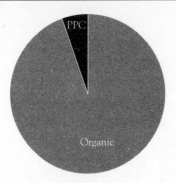

Figure 3.9   Which Kind of Search Results Are More Trustworthy?

takes to get ranked highly in competitive industries, you know how backward that sounds.

We all want our brands to be trusted. And now we have data showing us a new way to provide a trustworthy signal.

Of course, a lazy marketer might look at the graph in Figure 3.8 and think that the same trust advantage can be gained by simply buying his or her way to the top of the paid search engine listings. And I'd love to be able to tell you that would work; it's certainly easier than getting organic results.

So I asked survey takers, "Which kind of search results are more trustworthy?" And the vast majority of them told me that they trusted organic search engine results more than paid (pay per click [PPC]; Figure 3.9). That's kind of a bummer for marketers who have more money than time, but for the rest of us, it's an opportunity.

Want to get higher rankings and more trust? Spend some time creating awesome content and sharing that content in social media to attract links. All worthwhile modern content management systems are search engine spider–friendly. The technical aspects of SEO have been solved for you. Most companies not in super-competitive online spaces (such as pills, poker, and porn) don't need to hire SEO professionals. They need to hire content creators.

To dig deeper into paid search engine listing behavior, I asked survey respondents, "How often do you click on paid search engine results?" Around 60 percent responded either "never" or "less than

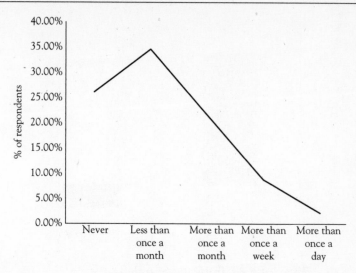

Figure 3.10   How Often Do You Click on Paid Search Results?

once a month" (Figure 3.10). So not only do searchers trust PPC results less than organic results, they also tend to click on them much less often.

If you have more money than time, more budget than brains, PPC is useful. For everyone else, PPC is something that should not be relied on. Experiment with it, sure, but don't neglect the much more valuable organic listings just because you can easily buy expensive AdWords traffic.

When I looked at our data from thousands of HubSpot customers, I found an interesting pattern that serves to justify the use of paid traffic, including PPC ads.

I analyzed days on which websites got more above average (for that site specifically) paid traffic and those days on which they got less than average, and I looked at the amount of organic traffic that those sites got on those days (Figure 3.11).

I found that on days with high paid traffic, organic traffic was also up over the site's average. And on days with lower-than-average paid traffic, organic traffic was also down. These data shouldn't be taken as a direct causation, but rather a correlation that demonstrates the holistic effect of online marketing. Nothing on your website

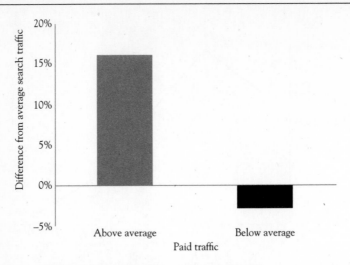

Figure 3.11   Effect of Paid Traffic on Search Traffic

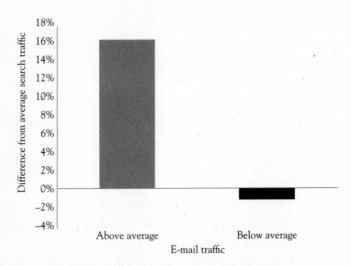

Figure 3.12   Effect of E-Mail Traffic on Search Traffic

happens in a vacuum. Don't be afraid to experiment with paid traffic sources occasionally and measure the effect they have on other traffic streams.

I also did a similar analysis with e-mail traffic, comparing days with above-average e-mail traffic to those with below-average e-mail traffic and their relationship to organic search traffic (Figure 3.12).

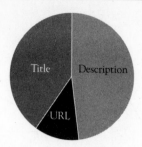

Figure 3.13   How Do You Determine Whether a Search Result Listing Is Relevant to What You're Searching For?

And here, too, I found a positive relationship. We notice this effect very strongly at HubSpot; on days we send high-performing e-mail marketing campaigns, we get more organic search and direct type-in traffic.

E-mail and paid marketing serve to put you at the top of your potential visitor's minds. And when you're top of mind, visitors are much more likely to click on your search engine results.

When I use search engines to find information, I type in a few words, scan through the results quickly, and if nothing catches my eye, do another search and repeat my scan. Usability expert Jacob Nielson calls this information foraging. Web users root around the Web like truffle-hunting pigs sniffing with our eyes for content that gives off the scent of being relevant to what we want.

Each search engine listing has three main kinds of text on the search engine results page with which to give off the scent of relevant content: the title, the description, and the URL fields. In my survey, I asked a multiple-choice question: "How do you determine whether a search result listing is relevant to what you're searching for?" I expected the title to be the most important factor, but nearly half the respondents reported relying more on the description (Figure 3.13).

This means that content creators need to think about the content on the page not only in terms of keyword relevance and spider friendliness but also in terms of real humans. Will that content give off an enticing scent and encourage readers to click?

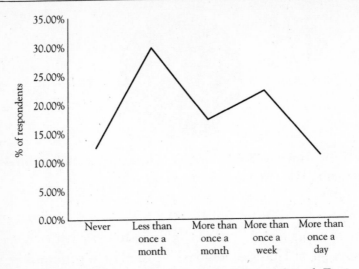

Figure 3.14   How Often Do You Encounter Spam in Search Engine Results Listings?

When I'm scanning a search engine results page, I often see a lot of content I consider spam, but I'm a marketer with a background in SEO and that may say more about me and what I expect to see than the reality. So I asked my survey takers, "How often do you encounter spam in search engine results listings?"

The results were more or less evenly distributed between "never" and "more than once a day" (Figure 3.14). But although just over 40 percent of searchers report seeing spam "less than once a month" or "never," more than 30 percent report seeing it at least "more than once a week."

Search spam exists, and normal searchers know it. Most of them see it on a regular basis. Your search engine results listing is right next to it. If you're writing too much for spiders, with keyword stuffing, repetition, and awkward grammar, you'll become just another spam listing. Write for humans first, and the rest will mostly take care of itself.

When I think of writing for search engine spiders, I think of long, keyword-rich page titles. Writing for humans generally means shorter, punchier headlines.

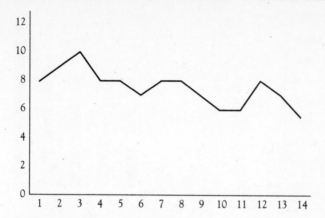

Figure 3.15   Effect of Title Length on Links

Diving into the SEOmoz data again, I compared the number of inbound links pointing at tens of thousands of pages on the Web and the length of their titles. I found that as title length increased, there was a slight decrease in inbound links (Figure 3.15). This does not mean you should be deathly afraid of writing verbose headlines, but it does mean you should not be married to the idea that you need to put every single keyword that you can possibly think of in every title tag on your site. Again, write for humans; the search engines have gotten smart enough to find the best content.

Then I looked at specific words in the titles of the URLs in the SEOmoz data set and their relationship to the number of incoming links those pages had. To ensure statistical significance, I looked at only very common words, so most of the most linked-to words in Figure 3.16 are very mainstream and somewhat generic words.

The perennially powerful *free* is among the top words, showing us that the power of free stuff knows little bounds. Also at the top are the words *news* and *breaking*, belying the power of novelty and new information.

A more subtle, but useful point is the occurrence of the word *photo*. Next to the word *video* it indicates that multimedia content is a favorite of the linkerati, but when we look at Figure 3.17, we see it also exemplifies another phenomenon.

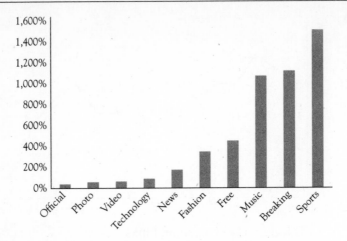

Figure 3.16   Most Linked-To Words

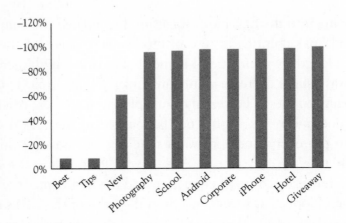

Figure 3.17   Least Linked-To Words

Here on the flip side of the coin, with the least linked-to words, we find those common words correlated with pages having a lower-than-average number of links pointing at them. Notice the word *photography*. A page that uses that word is likely about the art or technology of taking photographs and is aimed at a niche audience of photographers. In contrast, the word *photo* indicates that the page is full of pictures, something which nonphotographers can also enjoy.

4

Twitter

TWITTER IS MY favorite social site. I love the simplicity, the flexibility, and the vast audience. I remember a time before the word *retweet* existed, when it took only 30 or so tweets from about as many people for a phrase to become a trending topic worldwide. It is the perfect platform for the distribution of marketing content. Describe a link, paste it in the box, and hit Tweet. Your followers can then click and read, and if they're so motivated, they can share that link with their followers. It's the most elegant viral mechanism yet invented.

I hold some controversial points of view about Twitter, but none without data backing them up. And that's what this chapter is—my most important Twitter data (and the best collection of it anywhere).

I've long been interested in the idea that "engaging in the conversation" is the single most important function of social media marketing, so I've applied my analysis to test that statement in a variety of places. One of those places has been Twitter.

I looked at millions of Twitter accounts and separated them into two groups: those with more than 1,000 followers (the first light-colored bar in Figure 4.1) and those with fewer than 1,000 followers (the first black bar in Figure 4.1). I then compared those two groups by the percentage of their tweets that started with an "@" sign to arrive at a reply percentage. I repeated this analysis with accounts having more than 1 million followers (the second light-colored bar in Figure 4.1) and accounts with fewer than 1 million followers (the second black bar in Figure 4.1) and found similar results.

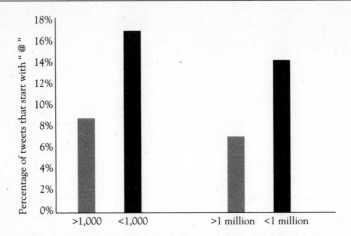

Figure 4.1   Reply Percentage and Follower Count

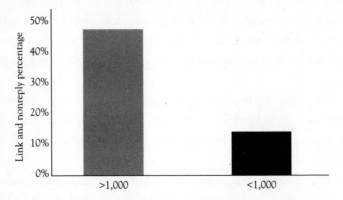

Figure 4.2   Highly Followed Accounts Tweet Lots of Links

Highly followed accounts tend to spend a lower percentage of their tweets replying to other accounts—they are less conversational—than less followed accounts.

The first question I thought when I uncovered the data in Figure 4.1 was, "If they're not engaging in the conversation, what are they doing?" So I did the same breakdown of more than 1,000 versus fewer 1,000 followers—but this time I analyzed the percentage of tweets that did not start with an "@" sign and that contained a link (Figure 4.2). I measured how much content was being broadcast by these accounts.

I found that highly followed accounts tweet more links than their lesser followed counterparts. These accounts did not build their reach by being in conversations; they built it by sharing interesting content in a broadcast fashion. In fact, there are not many examples of well-known Twitter accounts that are built on lots of replies, whereas there are countless accounts with more than 1 million followers that do nothing more than share interesting facts, quotes, links, and news.

Do not think of "engaging in the conversation" on Twitter as a way of building your reach. Instead, focus on gathering and sharing as much interesting, relevant content as you can.

If you should tweet lots of links to get followers, how many links is too much? Is it possible to overtweet?

Using data from HubSpot's free Twitter Grader tool, I analyzed just over 5 million Twitter accounts and compared the number of times per day they tweeted on average and their number of followers (Figure 4.3). I found that followers peaked with accounts that

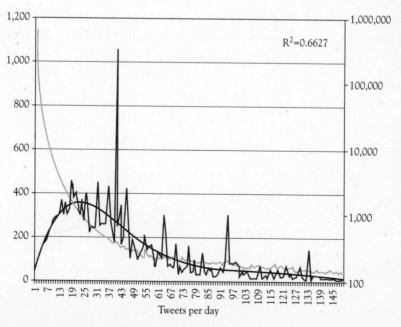

Figure 4.3   Tweets-per-Day versus Followers

tweeted around 22 times per day and there was no steep drop off beyond that.

Twenty-two tweets per day, on average, is a pretty breakneck pace for most accounts to keep up, especially if they're tweeting interesting content and not just anything they find. The takeaway of this graph is not that 22 times a day is a magical number, just that it's pretty hard to overtweet. And if you're wondering how often you should tweet, the answer is generally "more than you currently are."

During my research into Twitter, I translated two linguistic analysis systems to the microblogging platform: Linguistic Inquiry and Word Count (LIWC) and Regressive Imagery Dictionary (RID). I did not invent these two systems; they were created by academics at universities. I simply applied them to social media.

One of the traits that these systems allowed me to analyze was self-referential language—how often accounts refer to themselves, either as individuals or as an organization. This includes use of words such as *I*, *me*, *us*, and *we*.

When I compared the percentage of tweets that used self-referential language to the number of followers those accounts had—looking at millions of accounts—I found a striking pattern (Figure 4.4). As self-reference increases, follower count decreases.

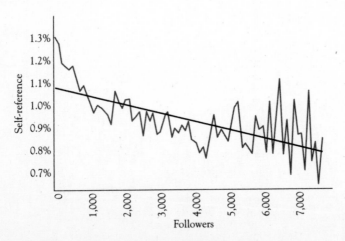

Figure 4.4   Effect of Self-Reference on Followers

For most noncelebrity individuals and brands, Twitter users do not follow them to hear them talk about themselves constantly.

Those same linguistic analysis systems also allowed me to look into the relationship between negative sentiment and followers. Here also, I found a similar, striking pattern. As negative remarks increase, follower counts decrease (Figure 4.5).

People don't go to social media to get bummed out about the world around them; they can just turn on the TV news if that's what they want. They go to social media to talk to their friends and generally feel good.

This sounds like unicorns-and-rainbows superstition, but in this case, the data support it. Negativity doesn't sell on social media as well as positivity does.

When you sign up to Twitter, you're given the ability to provide three bits of personal information: a profile picture, a 160-character bio, and a link to your home page. Over the years I've tracked the number of accounts that fail to fill these fields out, and although the numbers have gotten better with time, I'm still surprised by how many accounts don't take the few moments required to do this.

When I analyze the relationship between providing this information and follower counts, the results are unsurprising. In all three cases, accounts that provide a picture, bio, and home page

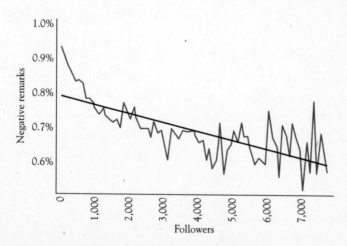

Figure 4.5   Effect of Negative Remarks on Followers

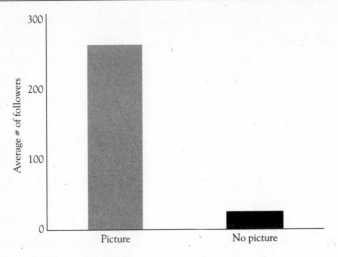

Figure 4.6 Effect of Profile Picture on Followers

link all have more followers than accounts that do not. Figure 4.6 shows the number of followers versus having or not having a profile picture, but the effect is the same with the other two fields as well.

Take the time to fill out your Twitter bio. Users want to know who you are before they'll follow you.

Going a step further, I dug into actual language used by Twitter account holders in their bios. One common unicorns-and-rainbows myth is that you should not call yourself a guru or use any other word to label yourself an expert.

But the data contradict this superstition. I found that Twitter accounts that used the word *guru* in their bios had about 100 more followers than the average account (Figure 4.7). These data do not mean that if you go over onto Twitter right now and add that word to your profile that you'll instantly get more followers. But if you look at the rest of the graph, it does indicate that you should not be afraid to identify yourself authoritatively. Tell potential followers why they should listen to you. If you've written a book, founded a company, or are an expert on something, tell us.

But remember the data about self-reference in tweets. The bio is the only place you should be talking about yourself.

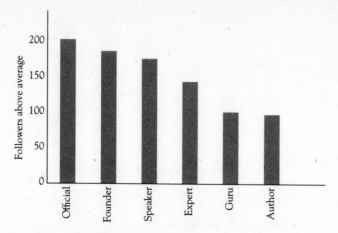

Figure 4.7   Effect of Bio Words on Followers

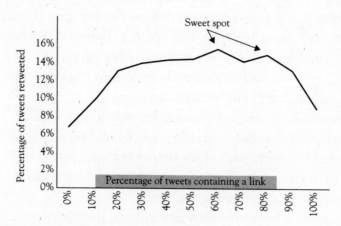

Figure 4.8   Sweet Spot for Retweets: Links

So far, I've presented data only about follower counts, but I've also spent a great deal of time analyzing retweets as well. In Figure 4.8, I compared the percentage of accounts' tweets that contain a link and their average number of retweets per tweet.

I found that here is a sweet spot of linking for maximum retweets. Accounts that posted 60 to 80 percent links tended to get the most retweets. Ninety percent or more links can look spammy, so retweet performance tends to drop off there.

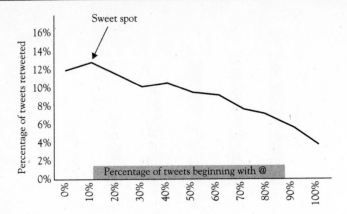

Figure 4.9   Sweet Spot for Retweets: Replies

Then I looked at a similar comparison of reply percentage and retweets and found a much different sweet spot (Figure 4.9). Basically, the more replying done by the Twitter accounts in my data set, the lower their average retweets per tweet.

As these data and the data about follower counts show, constantly replying and being chatty on Twitter does not benefit a marketer in terms of reach or content spread. If you're using Twitter as a marketing channel, with the goal of building a large audience of engaged followers who often share your content, you'll be best served by focusing on sharing a lot of interesting content, rather than replying to every message you get.

When I first began my retweet research, the easiest way I found to get more retweets was to simply ask for them (Figure 4.10). In fact I conducted an experiment before the word *retweet* had been invented where I simply asked people to tweet a certain link, and the title of the experiment ended up trending worldwide.

Over the years since then, I've had many discussions and debates about the power of asking for retweets. More recently, I decided to update and solidify my data about it to put an end to the doubt.

I looked at 20,000 randomly selected tweets and broke them into three groups: those that contained the phrase *please retweet*, those that contained *please RT*, and those that contained neither call to action. I found that whereas only 12 percent of the "neither"

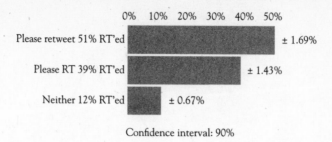

Confidence interval: 90%

Figure 4.10   Phrase *Please Retweet* Gets Four Times More Retweets

group's tweets were retweeted, more than 50 percent of the "please retweet" group's tweets were.

Calls to action work in all forms of marketing, and social media is no different. If you want more retweets, ask for them.

Thanks to the great people over at Buffer (an awesome app you should check out), I was able to study millions of tweets and their retweet performance. First, I looked at the relationship between the time of day the tweets were sent and how many retweets they got (Figure 4.11). The data confirmed my earlier analysis on a different data set and showed that retweets were highest for tweets posted between 3 PM and 5 PM Eastern time.

I know from personal experience that as the business day wears on, I often lose the motivation and wit to come up with worthwhile original tweets. It's around 4 PM that my retweeting activity increases because of this.

Experiment with tweeting those updates you want to spread during this time period and see if it works for you.

The first large-scale retweet data set I compiled was more than 100 million retweets gathered over the course of more than a year. It was this database that formed the basis of much of my earliest work on Twitter.

Using this data set, I was able to analyze the volume of retweeting activity that occurred on the different days of the week. I found that although overall Twitter activity tends to be highest early in the business week, retweeting peaks on Fridays (Figure 4.12).

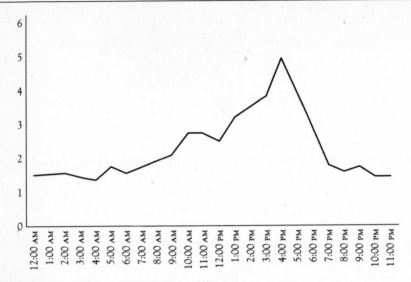

Figure 4.11   Time of Day versus Retweets

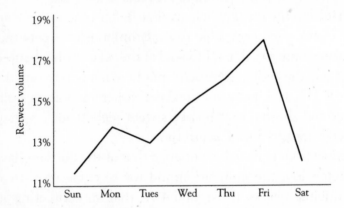

Figure 4.12   Retweet Activity by Day

I think the reasons for this might be similar to the reasons that the end of the business day is the best for getting retweets. And the tactical takeaway is much the same as well. On Friday afternoons, look over the content you've posted during the week and share the best stuff again. After a few weeks, you'll learn if Friday afternoon as a highly retweetable time works for your business and your audience.

Earlier in this chapter, I included data that showed that self-reference was correlated with lowered follower counts. I also analyzed the relationship between self-reference and retweets and found a similar pattern (Figure 4.13).

Looking at millions of retweets and millions of non-retweeted "normal" tweets, I found that non-retweets tended to contain more self-referential language than retweets. Not only does self-reference not lead to more followers, it also doesn't lead to more retweets.

When I share one of your tweets with my audience through a retweet, I need to believe that it will be relevant and interesting to my followers. The minutia of your life—what you had for lunch and how many times your cat farted—is very unlikely to make that cut. If you're on Twitter to communicate with friends you know in real

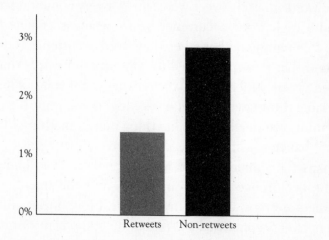

Figure 4.13   Amount of Self-Reference in Tweets and Retweets

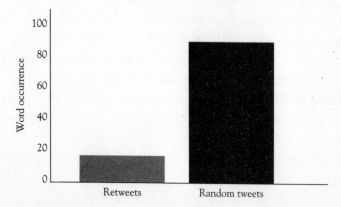

Figure 4.14   Word Novelty in Retweets

life, feel free to talk about yourself all day long, but if you're there for marketing and business reasons, stop talking about yourself.

Whenever I've asked people, in surveys or focus groups, why they retweet some tweets but not others, the idea of novelty comes up frequently. People tell me that they want to retweet new information (Figure 4.14). They want to be the first, not the last, to inform their followers of some breaking news. Scarce and new information is valuable information. Things that everyone else knows aren't particularly worthwhile.

In an effort to quantify this idea, I looked at word occurrence in retweets and non-retweeted normal tweets. I measured how common the words in each tweet were (*the* is a very common word and thus had a high word occurrence score, whereas *sesquipedalian* is much less common and has a very low word occurrence score).

I found that retweets tended to contain rarer words than non-retweeted tweets. Nobody wants to retweet you if you're simply saying the same things everyone else is saying. If you want me to share your content, you need to say something new, something I (and my followers) haven't heard—or read—before.

Perhaps the simplest bit of retweet analysis I've conducted is about the occurrence of links in tweets and the likelihood that those tweets are retweeted. In my data set, I found that only 18.96 percent of tweets contained a link, but 56.69 percent of retweeted tweets contained a link. People are more likely to retweet a link rather than just a simple tweet (Figure 4.15).

These data should serve to reinforce the importance of sharing as many interesting, relevant links on Twitter as you can. Share your content—and don't be afraid to share it a few times—and find content from other sources that will also interest your audience and share those links. Establishing yourself as a source of useful, novel content is the most data-supported strategy to more followers and retweets.

I then analyzed the most common words and phrases that occurred in retweets more than they're expected to, based on how often they occur in non-retweeted normal tweets (Figure 4.16). I found a number of interesting things, but we should remember to

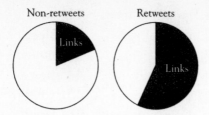

Non-retweets   Retweets

Figure 4.15 Effect of Links on Retweets

1. you
2. twitter
3. please
4. retweet
5. post
6. blog
7. social
8. free
9. media
10. help
11. please retweet
12. great
13. social media
14. 10
15. follow
16. how to
17. top
18. blog post
19. check out
20. new blog post

Figure 4.16 Most Retweetable Words and Phrases

think about the reasons why these words are on this list, rather than blindly using them and expecting more retweets.

The most retweetable word in my data set was the word *you*. Twitter users want to hear you talk about them, not yourself. The words *twitter* and *social* indicate that talking about social media in general and Twitter in specific works on Twitter. Also on the list are *please retweet* and *new blog post*, which corroborate earlier points about asking for retweets and the importance of novelty. *Free* is always a powerful word in marketing, and on Twitter it is no different. And we find *how to*, *top*, and *10* on this list, showing that utility content and chunked, list-based content performs well on Twitter, as it does on other forms of social media.

On the flip side of the coin, we find the least retweetable words, those words that occur far less in retweets than their commonality

1. game	11. well
2. going	12. sleep
3. haha	13. gonna
4. lol	14. hey
5. but	15. tomorrow
6. watching	16. tired
7. work	17. some
8. home	18. back
9. night	19. bored
10. bed	20. listening

Figure 4.17   Least Retweetable Words

in normal tweets would seem to predict (Figure 4.17). This list of words is far less interesting than the list of most retweetable words, and that's the point: they're boring.

Most of these words indicate that the person using them is talking about himself or herself and personal activities, such as watching the game, listening to something, or going to bed. Even worse is the occurrence of the word *bored* here. If you're tweeting that you're bored, don't expect it to get retweets, as you're being quite boring yourself.

An analysis I did of 2.7 million link-containing tweets revealed an interesting pattern that has implications for all kinds of communications professionals working with Twitter. I looked at each tweet in my data set and identified those that were clicked on zero times but were retweeted at least once. I also identified those tweets that were clicked on but were retweeted more times than they were clicked.

I found that 14.64 percent of the tweets in my study were never clicked on but were retweeted and 16.12 percent of the tweets in my database had more retweets than clicks (Figure 4.18). This tells me that many people who will retweet an article will do so without reading it first.

Although the sociological implications of these data could certainly be quite interesting, I'm mostly interested in what this means for marketers. And what it means for marketers is that your headline is the most important piece of your content when it comes to

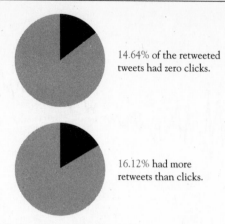

14.64% of the retweeted tweets had zero clicks.

16.12% had more retweets than clicks.

Figure 4.18   Retweets versus Clicks

Twitter success. If your headline doesn't entice and motivate the retweet, the body of your content might not ever get the chance to succeed.

Even if much retweeting happens in the absence of clicks, I'm still interested in getting people to click on the links I post to Twitter. When it comes time to leverage the huge reach and retweet counts we've built on Twitter into actual dollars-and-cents return on investment, it's all about how much traffic we can send to our website and then convert into leads or customers.

When analyzing clicks on Twitter, I use a metric called click-through rate (CTR). Marketers will be familiar with this from e-mail marketing or pay per click (PPC), but it functions a little differently on Twitter. I divide the number of clicks on a link by the number of followers the user had when they sent the tweet in question.

The first thing I looked at when I began to study Twitter CTRs was the length of the tweet, in characters. I found that longer tweets (up to about 130 characters) tend to get more clicks than shorter tweets (Figure 4.19).

Then I looked at the actual position within the tweets occupied by links and its relationship to CTR. Most Twitter users, myself included, typically put the link at the end of the tweet. The format is generally: "Title of the content: http://linktothecontent.com."

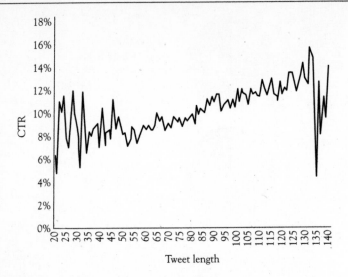

Figure 4.19   Longer Tweets Get More Clicks

Figure 4.20   Twitter CTR Heat Map

To visualize this data, I created the heat map you see in Figure 4.20. Each vertical bar represents a position of a link inside of a tweet. Bars to the left represent links placed at the beginning of the tweet; bars to the right indicate links placed at the end. The darkness of the bar represents the average CTR of the links at each position: the darker the bar, the higher the CTR.

My findings were surprising. Although there is a single dark bar at the end of the heat map, there is a much larger sweet spot of clicks about a quarter of the way into the tweet. After I first published these data, several people have told me that they've experimented with a format like "new post: http://linktopost.com title of the post" and it's worked for them.

I'm not sure why this format works so well; perhaps it's because most Twitter accounts are still putting links at the end of tweets, so tweets like this stand out. Experiment with it and see if it works with your audience.

I also analyzed the CTRs of 20 highly followed Twitter accounts, including mainstream news sources, such as the *Washington Post* and the *New York Times*; geekier sources, such as Mashable and Gizmodo; and celebrity accounts, such as the Kardashians and Alyssa Milano. I found that there is no standard CTR, as they vary widely across these accounts. The *New York Times* has a very low CTR, whereas Alyssa Milano has a very high CTR.

However, I did find one pattern that held true across all of the accounts I looked at. When one of them tweeted a link and didn't tweet another link for an hour, they had a certain CTR (Figure 4.21). When they tweeted two links in an hour, the CTR dropped. When it was three links in an hour, the CTR was even lower. As the pace of link-tweeting increased, the CTR for each link decreased.

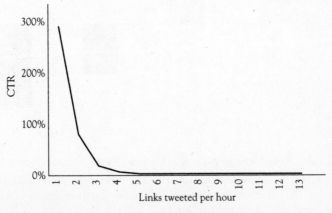

Figure 4.21   CTR by Links Tweeted per Hour

If you're sharing content you've found from other sources across the Web, tweet it as fast as you want. But when you're tweeting your own content to send traffic to your site, slow down and tweet it at a more deliberate pace.

Another CTR analysis I did was on parts of speech. I analyzed the four major parts of speech (adverbs, adjectives, nouns, and verbs) and their relationship to the CTR of the tweets they were found in. I compared the CTR of the individual tweets to the average for the Twitter user to account for the wild differences in CTRs.

I found that tweets heavy with adverbs and verbs performed better than tweets with more nouns and adjectives (Figure 4.22). Action-based words got more clicks than entity-based words. Action-based words include calls to action, which is likely the cause of some of this effect.

Don't forget to experiment with action-based calls to action on Twitter. If you want more clicks, ask for them. But be creative; don't just try "Click here," but instead try "Check this out" or "Tell me what you think."

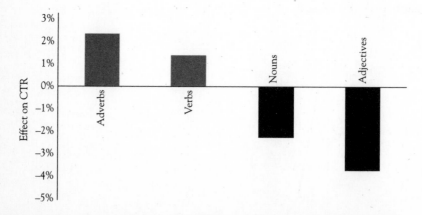

Figure 4.22   Relationship between Various Parts of Speech and CTR

Note: **Use action words: more verbs, fewer nouns.** After analyzing 200,000 link containing tweets, I found that tweets that contained more adverbs and verbs had higher CTRs than noun- and adjective-heavy tweets.

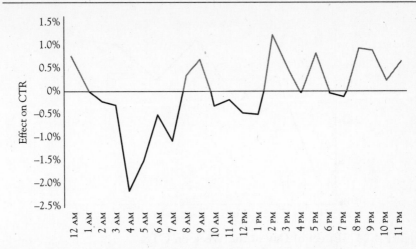

Figure 4.23 Relationship between Time of Tweet and CTR

Note: **Tweet later in the day.** I found that tweets posted in the afternoon hours had higher CTRs than tweets posted in the morning.

I also looked at the hour of data and its relationship to CTRs and found a pattern familiar if you think back to my data on retweeting and time of day.

Tweets posted later in the day—afternoon Eastern time— tended to have higher CTRs than tweets posted early in the morning (Figure 4.23). As with all timing data, be careful to test and experiment with these findings, as your audience may behave differently than the average of a very large data set.

And when I looked at the day of the week and its relationship to CTR, I found something surprising. Tweets that were posted toward the end of the week got more clicks than those posted on Monday through Wednesday (Figure 4.24). But it wasn't just Thursday and Friday that performed well; Saturday and Sunday also both have high CTRs.

I follow thousands of accounts on Twitter. My Twitter stream is very active during the business day Monday through Friday. On the weekends, it moves much slower, and what content does come through is often about sports and other non-work-related topics.

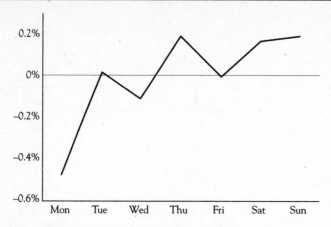

Figure 4.24 Effect of Day of the Week on CTR

The few times something interesting about marketing does show up on a Saturday or Sunday, it gets more of my attention because there are fewer other things fighting for it. I call this contra-competitive timing, and we'll see examples of it throughout this book.

Don't take these data to mean that you should tweet links only on the weekends. Instead, take it as an invitation to experiment with the weekends if you hadn't already been using them.

5

Facebook

FACEBOOK IS THE 800-pound gorilla of the social media space. The network has more than 1 billion active users around the world. Everyone is on Facebook: from the youngest to the oldest and from the geekiest to the most technology unsavvy. If you, as a marketer, had to pick only one social media channel to maintain a presence on, you'd have to go with Facebook.

Old-school marketers just waking up to this reality have been quick to jump on the advertising bandwagon and flood Facebook with mounds of ads with low click-through rates (CTRs). Although the targeting functionality of Facebook's self-service platform is quite powerful, advertising should be a distant second in the Facebook marketing priority list.

Your brand's Facebook page is its face (pun intended) to the social world. The content you share and the interactions you entice your fans to engage in define how well you'll do. This chapter will teach you the kinds of content and sharing behavior you need to understand to succeed.

The fundamental act of Facebook marketing is posting content to your brand's Facebook page. Hopefully that content then gets likes, shares, and comments, leading to a highly engaged audience, which you can then direct to your website to convert into leads or customers.

I collected a data set of all of the content posted by the 10,000 most liked pages on Facebook and the corresponding like, comment, and share data for each post. I began my analysis of this data by looking at the day of the week the content was posted and its

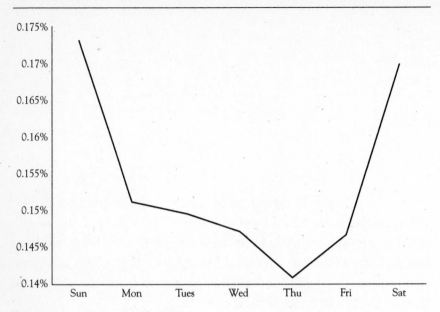

Figure 5.1   Days versus Likes

relationship to the number of likes it got (Figure 5.1). I calculated a like rate by dividing the number of likes on the post by the total number of likes for the page.

Echoing the contra-competitive timing pattern I've found elsewhere in my research and detailed in other chapters in this book, I found that content posted on Saturday and Sunday tended to get more likes than content posted during the business week.

I've said it before with other timing data, but it bears repeating here. Don't take these data to suggest that you should post content only on the weekend. Experiment with Saturdays and Sundays and see how it performs; you may be surprised.

Next, I moved on to study the time of day the content was posted and the relationship that had to the content's like rate (Figure 5.2). Here I found a pattern perhaps unique to Facebook and its place as a mainstream and largely nonprofessional social network.

Content posted in the evening, between 5 PM and midnight Eastern time, got more likes than content posted at other times during the day. For most people, Facebook usage at work is frowned on, and some data have suggested that many companies actually block

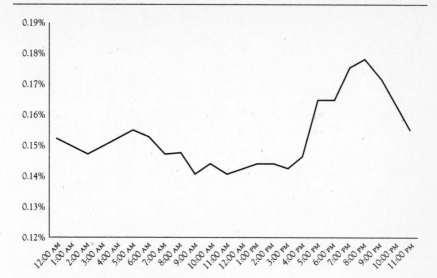

Figure 5.2 Hour versus Likes

access to it from the office. This means that much Facebook activity happens from home, after people get home from work.

Not only do these data suggest the importance of posting content outside of the workday, but it also reminds us that we, as marketers, are creating content to compete with real-world activities such as dinner, family life, and television—not just other work-related content.

When I looked at sentiment, I found a pattern mostly similar to what I've found in other forms of social media and online marketing: positivity works better than negativity (Figure 5.3). For these data I used a linguistic analysis system that gives content a sentiment score; positive numbers indicate positive sentiment, and negative numbers indicate negative sentiment. The size of the number in either direction indicates the strength of said sentiment.

One interesting way these data differ from my work on sentiment data from Twitter is that although positivity does perform better than negativity, negativity works better than neutrality. If you have a choice between negative and positive, generally you'll want to stay positive. But if that choice is between negative and neutral, go negative. Neutrality is boring, and boring is death on Facebook.

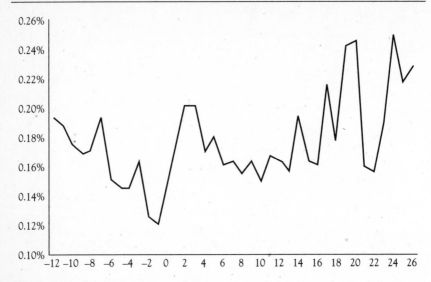

Figure 5.3 **Sentiment versus Likes**

One of the factors with the strongest relationship to a piece of content's like rate was the type of content. Facebook pages allow admins to post a variety of kinds of content, including photos, simple text-based status posts, videos, and links to external sites.

When I analyzed each post type and the average like rate, I found that photo posts performed the best, followed by status, video, and link posts, in that order (Figure 5.4). Facebook, for many users, is fundamentally a photo-sharing site. We post photos of ourselves, of our family and friends, of our pets, and of our dinner. It is only logical that we respond the most to brand content that is also visual.

In fact, at HubSpot, one of the most popular kinds of content we post to our Facebook page are "HubSpotter in the Wild" photos—candid shots of various employees at their desks. Users are on Facebook looking at photos of people; whenever you can, give them more to look at and like.

I then studied the relationship between the length, in characters, of the text of a wall post on the Facebook pages in my data set and the number of likes they got. I found that posts that were either very short or quite long did the best (Figure 5.5).

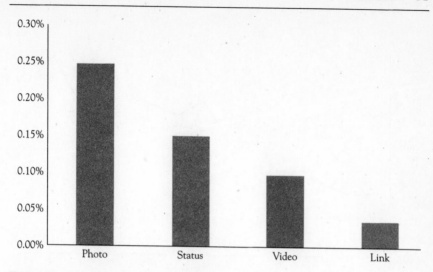

Figure 5.4 Post Type versus Likes

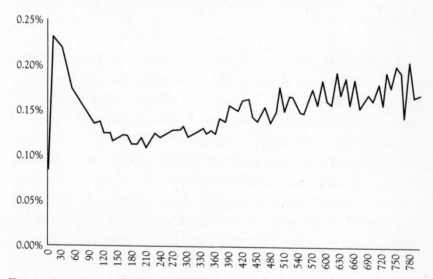

Figure 5.5 Post Length versus Likes

Again, we see that the middle ground is where performance drops. Posts between about 100 and 350 characters performed the worst. This is likely because Facebook users prefer to like photo-based content, which typically comes with only short captions. And if a post doesn't have an image and is primarily text-based, you're better off including a meaty amount of information, rather than a brief Twitter-length snippet.

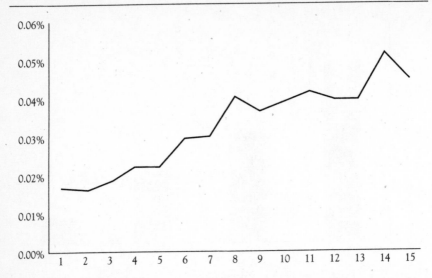

Figure 5.6   Self-Reference versus Likes

Another interesting way in which my Facebook data differ from my data on Twitter is when I analyzed self-referential language such as I, me, us, and we. On Twitter, talking about yourself and your brand can lead to fewer followers and retweets, but the same isn't necessarily true for Facebook. I found that as self-referential language increased in content posted to the Facebook pages in my data set, their like rate also increased (Figure 5.6).

Most Facebook users spend their time on the social network talking about themselves, telling their friends what they did today, posting pictures of themselves, and generally being self-referential. It makes sense that they're more tolerant of brands they've liked doing the same things their friends are also doing.

I'm a big fan of calls to action, and I often lament the fact that many marketers have become convinced that they don't have a place in social media. Nowhere is this more untrue than on Facebook. I analyzed posts that contained the word like and found that those posts had more than double the like rate of posts that did not contain the word (Figure 5.7).

Calls to action always work best in a persuasive or logical context. One of my favorite examples is the sports team whose Facebook

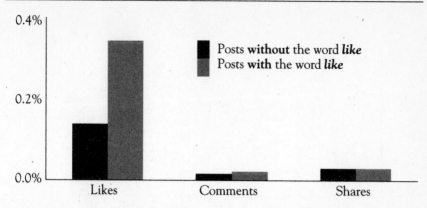

Figure 5.7   Posts Including *Like* Get More Likes and Comments

page contains posts talking about various awards and honors won by individual players. The posts ask viewers to like the post as a way to congratulate the players, and subsequently these posts are liked far more than the average post on those pages.

Experiment with different motivations to entice your readers to like your content, but don't forget to actually ask them to do what you'd like them to do—it works.

I then shifted my attention, in the same data set of 10,000 of the most liked Facebook pages, to the act of sharing rather than liking. I found several places where characteristics correlated with higher-than-average sharing were different than those associated with more likes.

One such place was in timing. Looking at the hour of day that posts were published, I found that sharing activity peaks much higher in the day than does liking activity (Figure 5.8). Posts published between 4 PM and 6 PM Eastern time had the highest rate of sharing (post shares divided by total page likes), with a sharp drop off later in the evening.

Another place where I found a difference between sharing-friendly behavior and like-friendly behavior was in the length, in characters, of the text of posts. Although very short, text-light posts tended to get the most shares, longer posts also attracted more shares than medium-length posts. (Figure 5.9).

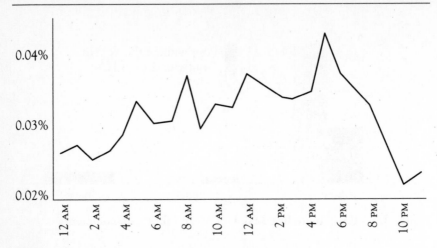

Figure 5.8   Share Percentage Based on Time of Post

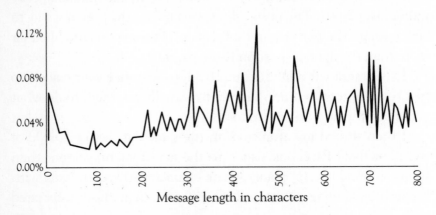

Figure 5.9   Share Percentage Based on Post Length

This is probably because the act of clicking Share involves a much higher level of commitment and engagement with content, so it requires more persuasion than a quick click of the Like button does.

As you're experimenting with your Facebook page, trying to increase the sharing your posts get, test some longer, text-heavy updates, providing your readers with plenty of motivation to spread your message to their Facebook friends.

The last place I found a difference between sharing and liking is in post type. Whereas for like rate for text-based content is the

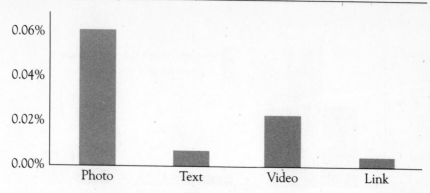

Figure 5.10 Share Percentage Based on Post Type

second highest performing type, when it comes to sharing, video posts perform better than text (Figure 5.10). Again, I believe this is because sharing a post with my friends is a much more involved action than just clicking Like, plus videos are a more immersive experience.

When compared with Twitter, Facebook tends to be a better place to share videos in social media. Twitter audiences are often multitasking, and asking them to spend 4 or 5 minutes watching only your video is a hard sell. Facebook, on the other hand, provides users with the ability to watch videos directly on the site, and users tend to be Facebooking when logged on, actively browsing the site, rather than just having it open in the background as then often do with Twitter.

If video production is a part of your marketing strategy (and you should at least test videos to see how they perform for you), use Facebook to promote them and think about how to encourage your viewers to share.

Continuing my investigation into the performance of calls to action on Facebook, I also looked at posts that contained the word *share* and their like, comment, and share rates. Not only do those posts get more shares than posts that don't use the word, but they also tend to get more likes and comments (Figure 5.11).

Again, don't forget the context of the social call to action. A great example of how to motivate sharing is to ask readers to share

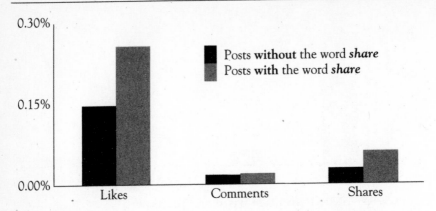

Figure 5.11 Posts Including *Share* Get More Shares, Comments, and Likes

a post if they agree with a statement you've made or if they can identify with an experience you're relating. A fitness page might talk about the moment when you can fit into jeans you had in high school and ask fans to share that post if they've ever been able to say that (or hope to be able to say it soon).

The third place I looked for evidence of the efficacy of social calls to action on Facebook was with posts that used the word *comment*. Here we find that the posts do get significantly more comments; they also get more likes, but they seem to get fewer shares (Figure 5.12).

It makes sense, in Facebook culture, to comment on a post and like it, but it's somewhat less natural to comment on and share the same post. This is especially true since most sharing activity actually includes comments added to the content by the sharers when it appears on their wall.

Easy ways to incite more comments are to use fill-in-the-blank posts and ask readers to finish your statement with a comment. A sports page could ask fans to fill in the best game they've ever watched. My favorite airline, JetBlue, did an experiment where they posted fill-in-the-blank updates for every week about the just-released *Hunger Games* movie.

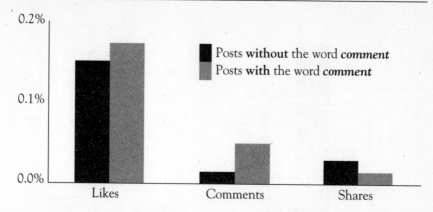

Figure 5.12 Posts Including *Comment* Get More Comments and Likes

Another way to drive increased comments is to use questions. But my data suggest that marketers need to be aware of the effect comments can have on other metrics such as likes and shares. Posts in my data set that included a question mark got more comments but fewer likes and shares than posts that did not include a question mark (Figure 5.13).

Likes are typically reserved for content that viewers agree with, things they literally like. Rhetorical varieties aside, questions are something you answer, not generally something you agree or disagree with. Periodically using questions to encourage commenting can work, but they're not an all-encompassing engagement panacea. Use them, but use them as part of an overall strategy.

I also dug deeper into the questions tactic to find out which kinds of questions led to the highest comment rates in my data set. I found that the easier-to-answer question types, such as *should*, *would*, and *which*, performed the best, whereas complex questions, such as *why* and *how*, drove the least comments (Figure 5.14).

Should and *would* questions are typically answerable with a simple yes or no. *Which* questions are generally presented as multiple choice, where readers merely need to select from a list of answers. *Why* and *how* questions require longer, well-thought-out answers and a larger investment of time from fans.

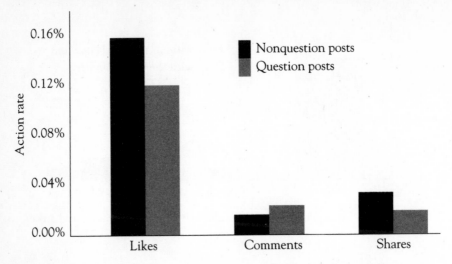

Figure 5.13   Question Posts Get More Comments but Fewer Likes and Shares

Note: Posts that include questions tend to get more response in the form of comments but fewer likes and shares.

When using questions to drive Facebook engagement, stick to the easy-to-answer varieties most of the time. The data show that these will do the most good for your page. But feel free to experiment with more in-depth questions to see how your audience reacts to them.

Perhaps the most interesting data I found when studying my commenting data was the relationship between post sentiment and the amount of comments posts had. On Twitter and in e-mail marketing, positivity does better than negativity. And when we're talking about likes on Facebook posts, positivity also comes out the winner. But when I looked at commenting, I found that highly negative posts drove more comments than positive posts (Figure 5.15).

This is quantitative evidence of the controversy hook often mentioned by social media thought leaders. Stirring the pot and challenging your readers with an opinion they might not agree with can be an easy way to rile them up and into action. Pointing out an evil done by a common enemy can incite an us-versus-them style of energy and drive up comments as well.

Certainly experiment with these kinds of edgy content, but do so carefully. Occasionally going negative can work, but you don't

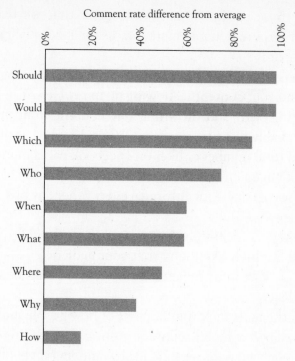

Figure 5.14 Certain Types of Questions Get More Comments

Note: Posts that include *should*, *would*, and *who* questions get more comments than those that include *why* and *how* questions.

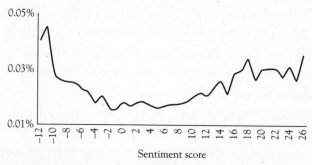

Figure 5.15 Comment Percentage Based on Post Sentiment

want a reputation as an exceedingly negative content producer or a constant Debbie Downer.

One of the most common questions about Facebook marketing that I'm asked when I speak at conferences is, "How often should we post?" When I'm asked that question about blogs, Twitter, or e-mail marketing, my answer is the same: "More than you are right now." On those platforms my data suggest that it's hard, if not impossible, for a reasonable marketer, using good-quality content, to go overboard.

Facebook is a different story, however. If you're posting too often to a page and your content is showing up in my News Feed, it might be competing with and drowning out content from my friends, which I probably want to see more. When I looked at posting frequency and total number of likes on Facebook pages in my data set, I found that fan count was the highest for pages posting between 0.5 and 0.6 times per day—roughly once every other day or 4 to 5 times a week (Figure 5.16).

Frequency is definitely something you should experiment with; there is a high likelihood that your audience varies from the average, but start your experimentation from this best practice frequency level.

One of the most important aspects of how people use Facebook is the prevalence of mobile content posting. I studied tens of thousands of publicly viewable posts made by random Facebook users and analyzed the applications they used to post that content. I found that even in late 2011, when I did this research, a full third of all content was posted to Facebook using mobile applications (Figure 5.17). This number has undoubtedly increased since then. The most common mobile application was m.Facebook.com, the mobile website, followed by Android, iPhone, and BlackBerry native apps. Note that this is content posting, not just content consumption, which has a much higher percentage of mobile activity.

The content you're posting to your company's Facebook page isn't competing only with your direct competitors or even simply other businesses' content. You're competing with pictures of my friends, my relatives, and their cute pets and babies. You're also competing with the real world, because there's a good chance I'm checking Facebook while out shopping or at dinner. Can your content stand up to that?

Facebook is such a mainstream network that there are millions of people of all ages interacting with it regularly. I analyzed data on millions of Facebook profiles gathered by HubSpot's free tool

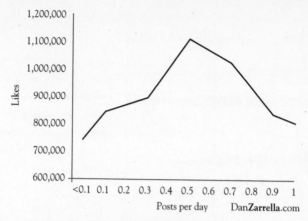

Figure 5.16 Effect of Posts per Day on Page Likes

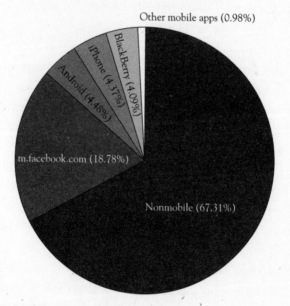

Figure 5.17 Mobile Facebook Posting Clients

Facebook Grader and found that the age of a user has an impact on how he or she uses the site (Figure 5.18).

The traditional social uses of Facebook, friend collection and wall posting activity, were highest for users in their teens and 20s. These young users had the most friends and wall posts. As the age of users increased, their use of the self-descriptive parts of the site

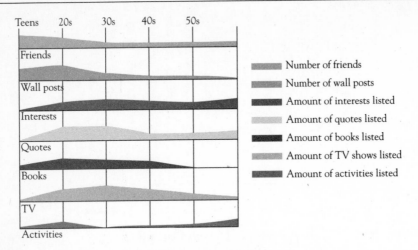

Figure 5.18   Facebook Profile Activity by Age

tended to also increase. Older users had more interests, quotes, books, TV shows, and activities listed on their profiles.

As marketers, this is a reminder that we must understand our audience and how they use Facebook, rather than simply assuming they use it the same way we do.

In the Facebook Grader data set, the average page had 624 fans. I analyzed the characteristics that were correlated with pages having higher or lower numbers of fans and found that one of the most detrimental was the presence of certain jargon and buzzwords (Figure 5.19).

Pages that used words such as *optimization, consulting,* and *productivity* tended to have far fewer likes than the average page in the data set. We know that most Facebook activity happens after business hours and that business content is competing with content from my family and friends, so it makes sense that boring professional words like these would perform poorly.

It is possible to communicate with Facebook users about their jobs and about topics like these, but we have to do so creatively and avoid the same boring words we use in our white papers and reports. Remember, this is Facebook, not the Testing Procedure Specification (TPS) report.

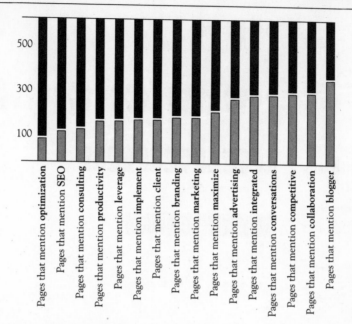

Figure 5.19   Effect of Buzzwords on Fan Count
Note: 624 = Number of fans an average Facebook page has

On the flip side of the coin, I found that there are certain words that are correlated with pages having more than the average number of likes in the Facebook Grader data set. An interesting set of these words were related to guilty pleasure–type foods. Pages that included the words *ice cream*, *chocolate*, and *sugar* tended to have many more likes than the average (Figure 5.20).

Think about it, which do you really like more: *integrated advertising consulting* or *chocolate ice cream*? Facebook is where users let their hair down, so you need to relax your corporate content and talk to users in a way that won't remind them of the inside of a cubicle.

When you create a Facebook page, you are asked to specify what type of page you're creating. In my data set, I looked at which of these types had higher-than-average numbers of total likes and found very telling results (Figure 5.21).

The top of the list is full of mainstream, entertainment-style page types. Movies, television shows, books, music, and athletes lead. This is the kind of content you'd find on the cover of the

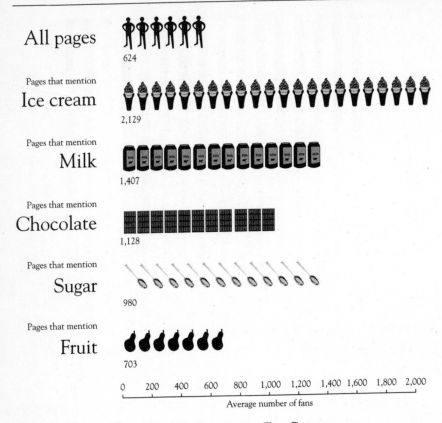

All pages
624

Pages that mention
Ice cream
2,129

Pages that mention
Milk
1,407

Pages that mention
Chocolate
1,128

Pages that mention
Sugar
980

Pages that mention
Fruit
703

0   200   400   600   800   1,000   1,200   1,400   1,600   1,800   2,000

Average number of fans

Figure 5.20   Effect of Food References on Fan Count

magazines at the checkout counter at the supermarket, the type of stuff you'd hear about if you turned on your television at prime time or listened to people talk at a bar next to you. This is normal people content, not geeky, corporate, or boring.

When thinking about content to promote your brand on Facebook, you need to think like a producer of this kind of content. How can you tell your story in a way similar to a blockbuster movie or a best-selling book? This will take a lot of experimentation and the biggest obstacle will be fear. Keep trying new things, and you'll start to understand exactly what your audience wants.

In Figure 5.22, we find the least liked page types—those page types that had fewer-than-average likes. This list reads like the most boring section of the yellow pages.

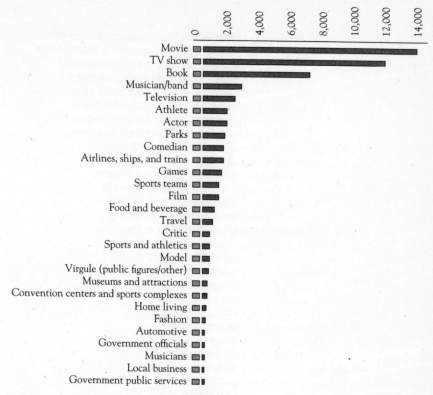

Figure 5.21   Most Liked Page Types

Financial services, professional services, and automotive dealers are included in this graph. This is not to say that these kinds of businesses shouldn't or can't use Facebook effectively, just that they need to try harder. If you're in one of these kinds of industries, it is especially important that you channel someone from a brand similar to the most liked page types graph. Think like a magazine editor, movie producer, or radio station DJ, and less like a real estate agent.

Although it sounds counterintuitive, it is possible for your brand's content to be successful on Facebook even if you don't have a Facebook page (although you should). This is true when the content you're publishing to your website is shared by viewers to their Facebook profiles, such as with the Like or Share buttons available to publishers. I compiled a data set of tens of thousands of articles

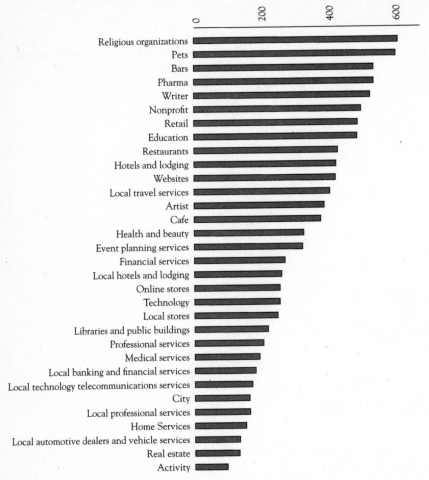

Figure 5.22   Least Liked Page Types

shared to Facebook to study the characteristics that were associated with sharing that was higher (or lower) than average.

Using the same two linguistic analysis systems I talked about in the Twitter chapter, I was able to find the content types that were most (and least) shareable (Figure 5.23). The most shareable kind of content was sexual content, but that's not really useful information for most marketers. What is useful to us is that the second most shareable kind of content is positivity and the least shareable is negativity. Here we find that for external content shares on Facebook, positivity and sex sell better than negativity or anxiety.

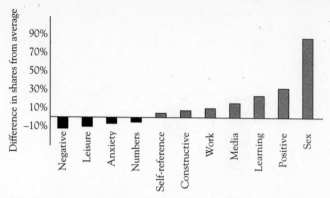

Figure 5.23   Linguistic Content Types and Facebook Sharing

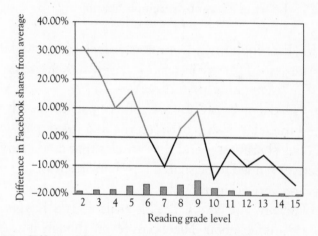

Figure 5.24   Effect of Reading Grade Level on Sharing

I also looked at the readability of the external content in my database. Readability is a measure of the complexity of a piece of content. The most well-known example is the Flesch-Kincaid measurement that is available in Microsoft Word. It produces a grade level that indicates the level of education required for a reader to be able to understand the text being measured.

I found that as the complexity of the language I analyzed increased, the number of times it was shared on Facebook by readers decreased (Figure 5.24). Readability measurements are largely based on the average length of words, in syllables, in the text. When

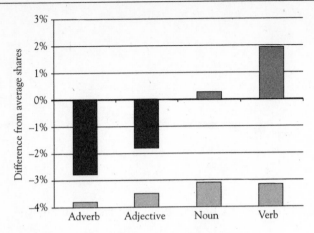

Figure 5.25   Effect of Parts-of-Speech on Sharing

writing for Facebook, avoid unnecessarily large words and write simply. Aim for a fifth grade reading level, rather than a twelfth. Think *USA Today* rather than *New York Times*.

Then I used a piece of software called a part-of-speech tagger to understand the relationship between the four major parts of speech and Facebook sharing. I found that articles that used many adverbs and adjectives tended to be shared less than articles that relied only on nouns and verbs (Figure 5.25).

One of my favorite books, *The Elements of Style*, has great advice for writers thinking about Facebook (even though it was written many years before Facebook): "Write with nouns and verbs, not with adjectives and adverbs. The adjective hasn't been built that can pull a weak or inaccurate noun out of a tight spot." Write plainly and simply.

Notice that I didn't say "write dumb." It is actually much harder and more stylistically sound to use simple and concise language. Work hard to write simply.

Finally, I looked at the most common words in the title of the articles in my data set and their relationship to sharing rates. Figure 5.26 shows the most shareable words list.

The word *Facebook* leads the pack, and one would expect it to. Facebook users like Facebook, so content about Facebook is naturally relevant. The rest of the list is mostly topics that were in the

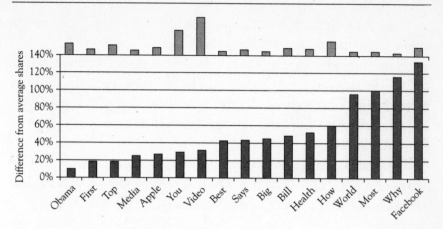

Figure 5.26   Most Shareable Words

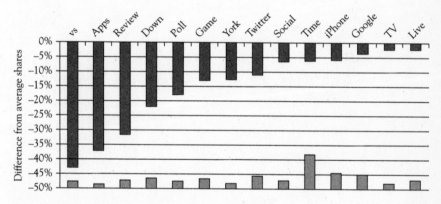

Figure 5.27   Least Facebook-Shareable Words

news around the time that I collected these data, topics you would hear about if you turned on the nightly news, such as the president and his health care bill. Facebook users are mostly interested in the same things everyone else is interested in.

Two notable exceptions are the prominence of the words *why* and *how* in the list. Facebook users seem to want more than short sound bite–style content. They want to read the story behind the stories they're hearing on the nightly news, not just the same things everyone else is saying.

The least shareable words list also provides some lessons for content creators aiming for Facebook success.

Here we find a variety of techy and geeky topics such as *Google*, *social*, *Twitter*, and *apps* (Figure 5.27). Facebook users are normal people; being on Facebook doesn't take an advanced computer science degree. And if Facebook users wanted to read about Twitter, they'd be on Twitter.

Do your best to avoid overly geeky topics or jargon when you're writing for Facebook. And if you're in a techy industry, experiment with relating your topics to more approachable ideas and stories.

6

Pinterest

PINTEREST IS THE newest social network that I cover in this book. Research done by other organizations, as well as my own experience, shows that it is very closely tied to purchasing behavior. Users have collections of products they want to buy or they want given to them as gifts. They have images of food they'd like to cook (and ingredients they'll need to buy). And they keep inspirational collections of clothing styles and accessories they want to wear. Clearly it's an important platform to investigate for use in your business.

The Pinterest API, however, is not public, and the ability to do qualitative research on the site is very limited. I was able to use search engine APIs and their cached copies of pages to collect a database of more than 11,000 pinned images and the number of times each was repinned, liked, or commented on.

This chapter is quite short, but Pinterest commerce-friendly usage and it's unique position as a visual content–based social network means that I still felt it was worth including these data.

The first characteristic about pinned content I analyzed was the length of the textual description attached to the image, in characters. An anecdotal glance over random pins tells me that short descriptions are best, but I'm not one to rely on gut feelings and small sample sets like that.

In my data, I found that repins were highest for images that had descriptions between 100 and 200 characters (Figure 6.1). This is similar to the length of a tweet, maybe a bit longer. Clearly the visual content is the focus of the show on Pinterest. The textual

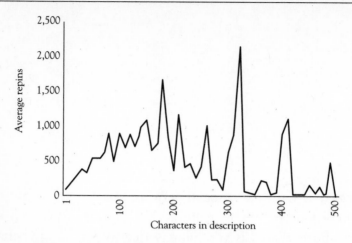

Figure 6.1   Effect of Description Length on Repins

content should be used to provide context, but the image itself should tell the story.

As I noted in Figure 6.1, the images are far more important than the text accompanying them on Pinterest, but it's far easier to analyze text to understand what is actually in the image it describes than it is to write code to analyze pixels of an image file to identify what it is. So that's what I did. I looked at my entire database of Pinterest data and found the words (excluding stop words such as *the* and *and*) that were most commonly found in descriptions (Figure 6.2).

If you've spent any time on the site, this list probably isn't very surprising. People enjoy pinning things they *love*, so that word tops the list. Other common areas of interest on Pinterest are *home* decoration (especially of the *DIY* variety), fashion and *style*, and *food recipes*.

If you work in an industry that deals with the topics on this list, awesome; Pinterest should be pretty easy for you. But if you don't, please do not take this list to imply that you have no place on the site. Start thinking of how you can blend the concepts listed here with what your business sells. A marketing company could use Pinterest to create a gallery of *inspiration* composed of its *favorite*

Figure 6.2   Most Pinned Words

brands. A sports brand could post *quotes* and talk about the best *products* and *places* to get fit.

Of course, the most commonly pinned words are interesting, but my favorite action on Pinterest is repinning. Similar to retweeting on Twitter or sharing on Facebook, it is the essential viral content spreading mechanism on the site. So I did an analysis where I found the common words that, when they occurred in the description of an image, were correlated with that image getting higher-than-average repins (Figure 6.3).

Here we find food dominating the list, specifically content such as *recipes* for *baked chicken* that only takes *minutes*. Quick, easy, and delicious food seems to be pretty popular. But the list also belies the guilty pleasure side of Pinterest—the less healthy *cake*, *chocolate*, and *sugar* also feature prominently here.

Outside of food references, which can be of somewhat limited utility for many marketers, we also find superlatives such as *top*, *favorite*, and *cool*. When you're pinning images, don't be afraid to tell readers why you love them enough to share them.

As you may have gathered from reading my data so far, I'm very interested in the relationship between conversation and other social

Figure 6.3   Most Repinnable Words

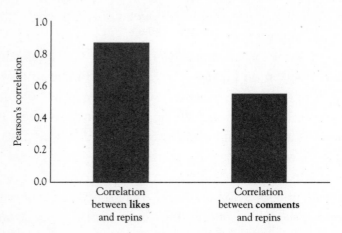

Figure 6.4   Correlation of Comments and Likes to Repins

metrics, such as views, retweets, likes, and shares. My Pinterest data set afforded me another opportunity to dig into that relationship.

I analyzed the correlation between likes of an image on Pinterest and the number of times it was repinned and the correlation between number of comments on an image and repins. As I also explain in the SEO chapter, a correlation score of 1 implies that the relationship between two numbers is perfect, whereas 0 tells us that there is no linear relationship between the two numbers.

I found that the relationship between likes and repins was much stronger than the relationship between comments and repins (Figure 6.4). The kind of content that motivates viewers to click Like is more similar to the kind of content that makes them want to share it than the kind of content that makes viewers want to comment.

If you browse Pinterest for a little while, you'll find images with a ton of likes and repins but very few comments, and the comments that it does have are short statements of agreement. On the other hand, you'll also see some with many commenters engaged in a heated debate over a controversial topic and very few likes and repins. I think for most marketers, it is more useful for their bottom line to strive for repins and likes rather than huge comment threads.

7

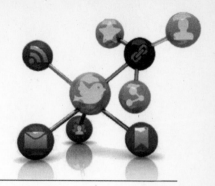

Blogging

I CONSIDER A blog the center of a content-based social media marketing strategy. Most content can be published as blog posts and then shared to social platforms. The general layout of a blog as well as the common software features make it easy to integrate with the rest of the social Web. Those visitors who find the content via Twitter, Facebook, or Instagram and follow it back to the blog can be prompted to subscribe to the blog via e-mail and become part of the audience sharing the next awesome piece of content your brand publishes.

But blogging isn't as sexy as it used to be. There are so many shiny, new technology tactics and social sites around that the lowly weblog has taken a bit of a backseat in terms of marketer mindspace. In this chapter, I'll present my body of research on blogging and how you can continue to use it effectively as the hub in your online marketing wheel.

As I often do when researching a new marketing channel or platform, I begin with a survey to understand the qualitative role that channel plays in the lives of users. When I started analyzing blogging, the first survey question I asked was, "How much do blogs affect your purchasing decisions?"

I've been a fan of blogging for many years. I started writing my first blog back in 2001, in fact. But even I was surprised by the importance of blogging for users gathering buying information. Close to 80 percent of my respondents answered "somewhat" or "very much" (Figure 7.1).

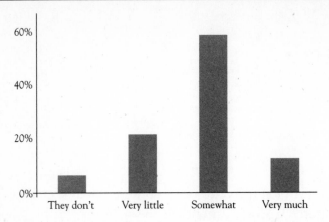

Figure 7.1   How Much Do Blogs Affect Your Purchasing Decisions?

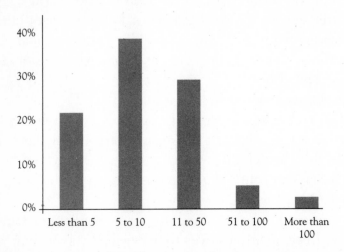

Figure 7.2   How Many Blogs Do You Read?

For most users, blogs play a not-insignificant role in purchasing decisions. If you're doing online marketing and you're not writing a blog, you'd better have a pretty good reason why not.

I then posed the question, "How many blogs do you read?" to survey takers. Just less than 80 percent reported reading five or more (Figure 7.2). Just a few years ago many Web users were reading blogs but didn't know they were as they weren't very familiar with the

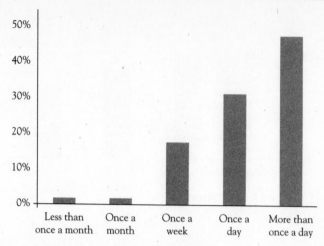

Figure 7.3   How Often Do You Read Blogs?

word. Now the majority of Web users are self-reporting that they read at least five.

Not only do you and your business need to be blogging, you need to remember that yours isn't the only blog your readers are consuming on a regular basis. No longer is it good enough just to show up to the blogging party. You must bring something unique and worthwhile to convince readers to give you time in their busy days.

And when I asked survey takers, "How often do you read blogs?" the picture of blogging overload became even clearer. Nearly 80 percent of my respondents reported reading blogs "once a day" or "more than once a day" (Figure 7.3).

Taken with the data from Figure 7.2, this means that most readers are reading five or more blogs at least once a day. Can you name the other blogs your audience is reading? Do you read them? Can you honestly say your blog provides information and content people cannot find elsewhere on the Web?

I know that my blog reading is kind of like newspaper reading. Or at least I assume it's like reading a traditional newspaper; being born in 1981, I'm too young to ever have done that regularly. I imagine folks waking up in the morning, pouring some coffee, and then poring over the day's news in the morning paper. That's

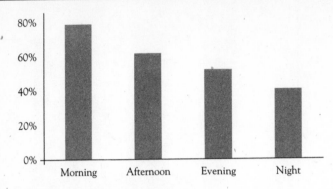

Figure 7.4   When Do You Read Blogs?

how blogs are. I get up, get to my office (or home office), fire up my blog reader, scan through the day's headlines, and stop occasionally when something catches my eye. Throughout the day, I may read another post or two, but they have to catch my eye somehow for that to happen.

When I asked survey takers, "When do you read blogs?" most echoed my behavior. Eighty percent reported reading them in the morning, with declining percentages as the day wore on (Figure 7.4). If you want people to read your blog regularly, be sure there is something new there in the morning for them.

In fact, when I analyzed 40,000 blog posts written by HubSpot customers, I found that data also emphasized the importance of morning publishing. When I looked at the average number of views for posts published at various hours of the day, I found that views were highest for posts published around 10 or 11 AM Eastern time (Figure 7.5).

This confirms the survey results in Figure 7.4, as well as my assumptions based on how I consume blog content. If you're blogging only once a day, do it in the morning.

But views are not the only reason to blog. Other important benefits of blogging are the inbound links that great blog content can attract to your site and the search engine optimization benefit those links to can bring.

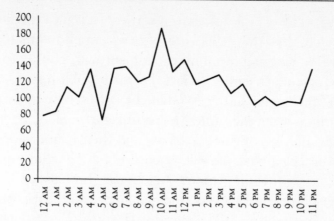

Figure 7.5   Views by Hour of Day

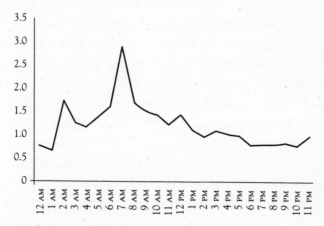

Figure 7.6   Links by Hour of Day

When I analyzed the hour of day blog posts were published and the number of links they attracted, I found something slightly different than when I was looking at views. I found that inbound links peak earlier in the day. Blog posts published around 7 AM Eastern time tended to have the most inbound links in my data set (Figure 7.6).

As I've mentioned in other chapters, not every Web user can create a link. It takes a certain, special class of users—folks such as bloggers, writers, journalists, and savvy social media users. Typically, these kinds of people are looking to get content up for that 10 or

11 AM viewership peak I described earlier. That means that in the hours before that, they're looking for new content to link to.

If you're blogging for links, experiment with posting earlier in the morning, much earlier. In fact, I actually publish my blog posts on DanZarrella.com just after midnight Pacific time to ensure my content is up when the earliest-rising linkerati are looking for it.

And when looking at comments and their relationship to the hour of day blog posts are published we find that they repeat the same morning-friendly pattern. Across the three major, postlevel blogging metrics, links, views, and comments, all the data tell us to publish our posts early in the morning (Figure 7.7).

As with all timing data, we must be careful to understand how to use it. These data are based on tens of thousands of blog posts across multiple industries. Your specific audience might differ from the averages presented here. If you're not currently publishing early in the morning, experiment by doing that a few times. If it works, great, keep doing it. If not, try a few other times.

Moving from hour of day to day of the week, I started by looking at the average number of views received by blog posts published on each day of the week.

Blog posts published on Monday tended to get the most views, and posts published on the weekend tend to have lower numbers (Figure 7.8). This differs from the contra-competitive timing

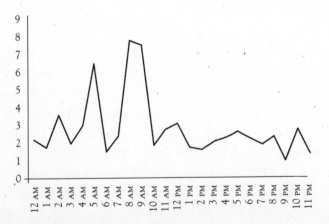

Figure 7.7   Comments by Hour of Day

phenomenon I've found across other marketing channels, but it doesn't mean you can't take advantage of both tactics. Publish your posts during the week, but experiment with promoting them in social media or through e-mail on the weekends.

When we look at incoming links and their relationship to day of the week, we find a pattern mostly similar to the views data. Posts published during the week (Monday and Thursday here) tended to have more incoming links pointing at them (Figure 7.9).

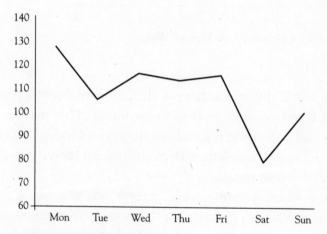

Figure 7.8   Views by Day of Week

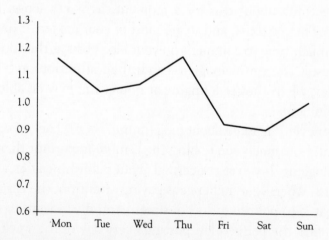

Figure 7.9   Links by Day of Week

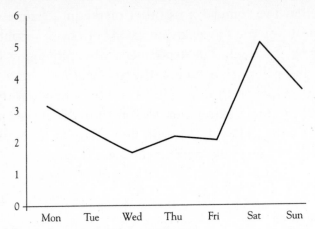

Figure 7.10   Comments by Day of Week

One subtle difference here is that Sunday doesn't perform as badly in terms of links as it does for views. This may be due to bloggers and journalists researching stories for Monday morning on Sunday. Again, experiment with publishing on these days and see if they work for your specific audience.

Here is where we see something surprising about blog post publishing days. Posts in my data set that were published on Saturday and Sunday received more comments than those posts published during the week (Figure 7.10).

If we think about this for a moment, it makes sense. During the week I'm very busy, and so are most of your readers. They don't have as much time to comment on your blog posts as they do on the weekends. If you can manage to catch their attention on Saturday or Sunday, when they're lounging at home, you may be able to get more comments.

Whenever I'm asked about blog timing, I come back to one central point: how much you're blogging is more important than when you're blogging. If you're concerned about publishing at exactly the right time, when your audience is paying attention, the easiest way to do that is to publish at lots of times. And if you want to experiment to find the perfect day, posting every day of the week makes that a lot easier.

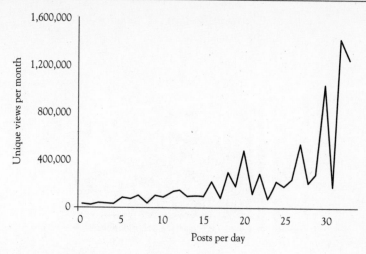

Figure 7.11 Unique Views by Posts per Day

When I analyzed thousands of the most popular blogs on the Web, I counted their average number of posts per day and compared it with the number of unique views per months they get (as reported by Compete.com). I found a distinct pattern. The more often those blogs published content, the more views they got (Figure 7.11).

I know this advice is borne out not only in the data but also in my experience both on DanZarrella.com and on the HubSpot blog. More blogging means more traffic. When I present these data, I'm often asked, "Okay, then how much should I blog?" My answer is always the same: "More than you are right now."

In my quest to challenge the "engage in the conversation" social marketing myth, I spent some time analyzing the correlation between comments on blog posts and the number of views and incoming links those posts got.

In both cases, I found there was an extremely low correlation between comments and views or links (Figure 7.12). In other words, the amount of conversation happening on your post has very little relationship to the number of people who see that post or the number of people who link to that post.

This means that marketers need to be clear about the reasons they're blogging. Are you doing it for traffic or links? Then don't worry so much about comments.

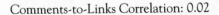

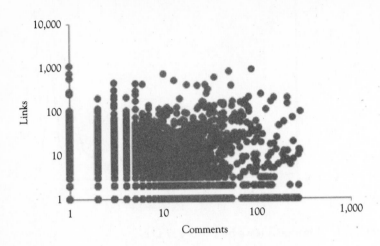

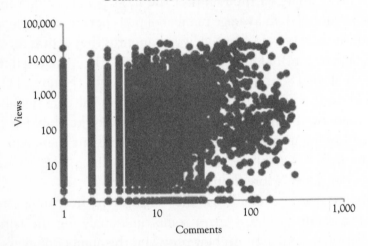

Figure 7.12 Comments-to-Links Correlation

I also analyzed the relationship between multimedia content in blog posts and the number of inbound links pointing at those posts and found that not all media content is created equal. In my data set, posts that included video had a higher than average number of incoming links, whereas posts with photos actually had fewer than the average number of links (Figure 7.13).

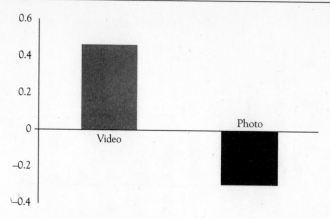

Figure 7.13   Links by Media Type

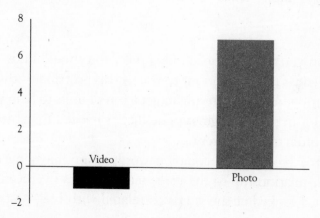

Figure 7.14   Comments by Media Type

I'm not exactly sure of the reasons for this, but we should take it as a signal to experiment liberally with multimedia content and closely measure its effect on our key metrics.

When I analyzed the same two kinds of multimedia content and comments, I found the reverse relationship. That is, posts with photos got more comments and posts with videos got fewer (Figure 7.14). Again, I don't have a great reason for this to be true, but it drives home the point that the factors that lead to more comments are often not the same as the factors that lead to increased performance in other metrics.

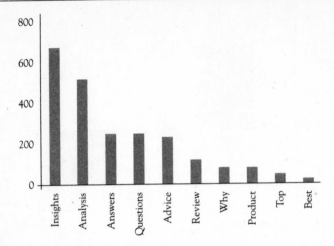

Figure 7.15 Most Viewed Words

When you're writing each blog post, you should know exactly what metric is most important to you. Is this post about stimulating conversation, or are you trying to get a ton of links to help your site rank better in search engines? The tactics needed to achieve each goal are often quite different.

Next, I broke down common words in my blogging data set and their relationship to the three main metrics I've been analyzing. First, I looked at the words correlated with blog posts getting higher-than-average views.

I found that words such as *insights*, *analysis*, and *advice* were near the top of the list of most-viewed words (Figure 7.15). Whenever I do a focus group or survey and I ask people why they read certain blogs or follow certain Twitter accounts, one of the most common answers I get is that they read them because they provide a unique point of view that the reader can't get anywhere else. Your readers don't necessarily want to hear you talk about yourself or your company constantly, but they do want to hear your unique analysis of the news. They want to hear you talk *as* yourself, not about yourself.

On this list we also find words such as *questions*, *answers*, *top*, and *best*. These indicate posts that are composed of content chunks— small, easily digestible bits of text, rather than huge paragraphs.

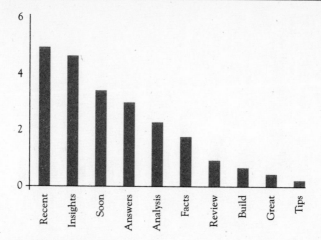

Figure 7.16   Most Linked-To Words

Frequently asked questions and answers and "top 10" and "5 best" lists typically take chunky formats.

On the list of most linked-to words we find several of the same words as on the most viewed words list, but we also find a few new appearances.

The words *soon* and *recent* are at the top of this list, indicating that the linkerati are concerned with linking to timely, novel, and potentially newsworthy content (Figure 7.16). Breaking as yet unheard news or discussing unfolding events before others in your space is a great way to attract links to your blog. When you can, act fast. At HubSpot we've had some of our greatest blogging successes by being agile and responsive.

Looking at the list of the most commented-on words, a pattern practically jumps out at us. Words such as *giveaway, jobs, gift,* and *money* dominate (Figure 7.17). Users will spend the time commenting on a blog post when there is something in it for them. Either they're entering a contest, trying to win a gift, or are interested in a job.

If you've decided that you need more conversation on your blog, the easiest way to accomplish that is by incentivizing it. Run a contest where readers enter by commenting and you'll be surprised by the number of otherwise silent users who come out of hiding to participate.

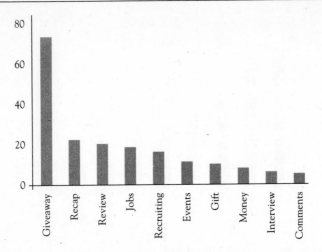

Figure 7.17   Most Commented-On Words

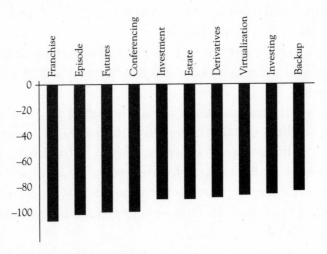

Figure 7.18   Least Viewed Words

The flip side of the high-performing words coin starts with a list of the least viewed words, that is, those words that correlate with blog posts getting less-than-average traffic (Figure 7.18).

I don't want to dwell on this list too long for fear of putting you to sleep, as the list is super-boring. Full of topics such as *franchise*, *futures*, *virtualization*, and my favorite *derivatives*, this list should serve as a warning to stay away from technical and unexciting jargon. Some industries will have to use these words on occasion, but if you do, you need to be careful to spice them up with something less boring.

The lists of least linked-to words and least commented-on words is nearly identical to this list, and printing all three lists would seriously endanger the attention span of my readers, so we'll avoid that. Suffice it to say that boring words don't help move any metric in the right direction and should be avoided at all costs.

PART

III

Middle of the Funnel (MOFU)

8

E-Mail Marketing

My RESEARCH INTO e-mail marketing began with several consumer focus groups designed to develop a qualitative understanding of e-mail user behavior and attitudes.

I began the discussion by asking about the first time attendees were exposed to and used e-mail. The most common answer had to do with school homework or business tasks. Throughout the focus groups, it became evident that "e-mail as homework" was a valid metaphor for understanding how users feel. It's a daily task they must accomplish and often don't relish. It's just something to get done and out of the way before they can move onto what they really want to be doing.

As a function of that metaphor, I found that the primary mode of user interaction with the inbox is filtering. They scan through the list of subject lines presented to them by their e-mail client, quickly glancing over each and deciding whether or not to open. Once they've opened it, they scan some more to decide to read and possibly take actions on the contents. In the case of nonmarketing e-mails, this is often a to-do item or a response. In the case of marketing e-mails, the user is deciding if he or she wants to click on the links presented.

Although the subject line forms the basis of the filtering criteria, the sender name also came up in the focus group discussions. Users were more likely to read and act on e-mails from names they recognized. And recognition came in two forms: people they know and celebrity names. Participants described a momentary and admittedly silly moment of surprise when they saw the president had e-mailed them personally asking for a donation. When sending mass e-mails, it's generally impossible to use a sender name personally known to each recipient, so marketers must rely on the celebrity name phenomenon if they wish to take advantage of the sender name. Well-known brand names, thought leaders, and actual media celebrities all work well for this.

Another common way users interacted with their inboxes was as a sort of archival system. They sent themselves reminder e-mails and often used search functionality to recall important information. They preferred e-mail conversations to voice when they wanted to have a retrievable record of talks. Include facts, figures, charts, and specific and periodically useful information in your e-mails to encourage users to search for and reuse them in the future.

Whenever I present marketing data, one of the most common questions I get is about the difference between marketing to business-to-business (B2B) and business-to-consumer (B2C) audiences. Many times people assume that social media marketing, or the more fun elements of traditional online marketing, are relegated to the consumer-facing world.

In one survey I conducted that reviewed e-mail behavior, I asked respondents if they used separate work and personal e-mail inboxes. Eighty-eight percent of respondents said no (Figure 8.1). This result is echoed in the focus group research I've done as well. Users tend to have a single point of collection for both professional and personal e-mails.

Your e-mail messages are appearing alongside not only other work-related information but a variety of more entertaining social

Figure 8.1   Do You Use Separate Work and Personal Inboxes?

e-mails as well. You are not competing against only other communications professionals trying to sell products or services; you're also competing against friends and family. Readers are scanning past your e-mail to find baby photos and party invitations. How well do you think your jargon-filled subject lines are going to fare in that kind of environment?

Perhaps the biggest change to e-mail consumption behaviors has come from the ubiquity of smartphones and tablet computers. I asked survey takers if they regularly checked their e-mail on mobile devices, and nearly 81 percent of them reported doing so (Figure 8.2). This does not mean that 81 percent of e-mail reading activity happens on phones, but it does mean that for the majority of your audience, receiving your e-mail while on the go is a very real possibility.

Beyond the technical challenges of ensuring your e-mails are optimized for mobile readability, you must contend with readers unchained from their desks. When the desktop or laptop leash is untethered, attention spans for reading boring commercial e-mails drop significantly. Your readers are grocery shopping, having dinner, or hustling through a busy airport when they're reading your e-mail now. Even if you've managed to get a subscriber to skip past an e-mail from a friend to read your newsletter, how much value is she going to get when she's splitting her attention between her phone and her lunch?

Marketers often tell me their biggest e-mail marketing challenge is list building. They want to know how to get more subscribers. To

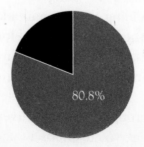

Figure 8.2   Most Users Report Reading E-Mail on Mobile Devices

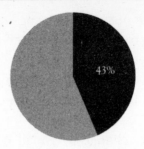

Figure 8.3   Percentage of Respondents Who Mentioned *Deals/Offers*

get an answer, I directly asked consumers why they sign up to get e-mails from companies and websites. And I asked through a free-form entry box so that respondents were free to write, in their own words, about their motivations. One of the most common categories of responses was that they were signing up to get a free product, a discount on a purchase, or some valuable content they wanted. Forty-three percent of survey takers said something to this effect (Figure 8.3). To them, subscriptions are a way to hook up to a nozzle delivering stuff they want on a regular basis.

This should come as no surprise to marketers, and it presents a fairly handy mechanism for list building. Find out what your visitors want from you—why they came to your site is a pretty good place to start—and give it to them in exchange for their e-mail address. Think about your e-mail marketing the way your subscribers will: as a way for you to give them what they want.

An interesting caveat to the "deals/offers" survey response type was that a significant portion of those users specifically said they would sign up only if the thing they were being offered was available only by providing their e-mail address. Twelve percent of respondents said they were looking for e-mail-only special offers, discounts, deals, and content (Figure 8.4). They want to be treated like VIP insiders and get special access unavailable elsewhere.

When you're designing the value delivery mechanism of your e-mail marketing, be sure you're offering something exclusive. And be sure you're communicating the exclusivity of your offer well. Tell

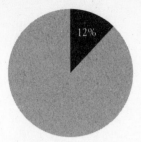

Figure 8.4   Percentage of Respondents Who Mentioned *Exclusivity*

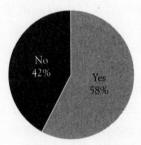

Figure 8.5   Do You Use a Separate Junk Inbox?

your readers that they're getting something special from you. If your readers can get your offer somewhere else, without giving up their e-mail address, why wouldn't they?

Although most of my survey respondents told me they did not have separate work and personal e-mail inboxes, 58 percent of them reported having a separate junk e-mail inbox (Figure 8.5). Typically these are accounts on free e-mail providers such as Yahoo!, Hotmail, or Gmail that users use only when they're giving their e-mail to companies whose e-mail they'd rather not see on a regular basis. In focus groups, I heard countless versions of the same story: a website is offering something in exchange for an e-mail address, so the visitor provides their spam e-mail address, checks it once to claim the offer, and then doesn't log in again until there's something else he or she wants from another website.

Providing a one-off offer of value is a pretty easy way to ensure you get the fake address. To avoid getting the junk mail wave-off, you must convince your subscribers that you'll be sending them

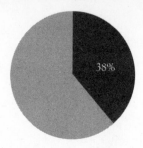

Figure 8.6 **Percentage of Respondents Who Mentioned *Relevance***

something of value regularly. Give them a reason to want to see your e-mails frequently and make sure they know they'll be disappointed if they miss one because they sent you to their spamme@ hotmail.com account.

The other most common response type given by survey takers when asked why they subscribe to e-mails from companies and websites centers around "relevance." Thirty-eight percent of respondents either used the word *relevance* or expressed a very similar concept (Figure 8.6). One particularly well-worded answer said that the writer signed up for e-mails they expected would be particularly and specifically interesting to them.

When you e-mail your subscribers, you're probably not actively trying to be irrelevant. You're sending them information related to what your company does or sells, and since they opted in to receive messages from your company, it's easy to assume all of your messages will be relevant. Many companies serve a variety of audiences with diverse motivations. Each reader probably wants something slightly different from you than every other reader.

The solution to the relevance problem isn't spending hours trying to make your monthly e-mail newsletter be more relevant to all of your subscribers. It's segmenting your subscribers into groups based on their interests and sending them different e-mail messages, each representing that facet of your company that they are particularly and specifically interested in.

When I analyzed HubSpot's customers' use of e-mail subscriber lists, I found that there was a difference in the performance of e-mails sent by companies that used multiple lists compared with

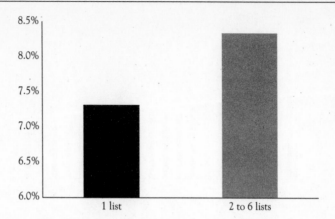

Figure 8.7   CTR by Number of Lists

those companies that used a single catchall list. Those companies that segmented their subscribers into two to six different lists had a mean click-through rate (CTR) 1 percent higher than that of companies that did not use segmentation (Figure 8.7).

When visitors come to your site, they should find a variety of ways to trade their contact information for some offer of value. The offer that speaks to a visitor tells you exactly what that visitor is interested in. Segment your subscribers based on the offer that got them to sign up to your list and send them e-mails related to that specific and particular interest.

I also analyzed the content of hundreds of thousands of e-mails sent by HubSpot's customers to find the characteristics of those e-mails that were correlated with having higher-than-average (or lower-than-average) CTRs.

One such characteristic was the language of the subject lines. I found a set of 20 words that were both common (occurred in hundreds of different e-mail) and correlated with higher-than-average CTRs (Figure 8.8). I'm not presenting this list as a checklist of words you must include in your subject lines. And, of course, simply adding one of these words to an otherwise bad e-mail won't instantly make it get more clicks. Use the list of words in Figure 8.8 as a guide to understand the kinds of ideas that make subscribers

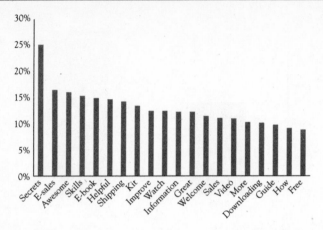

Figure 8.8   Most Clicked Lead Nurturing Subject Line Words

open and click e-mails. For each word, we should ask ourselves, why is this word here?

A quick glance at the list reveals a number of words that indicate the e-mail contains an offer of value for the receiver. Words such as *secrets*, *e-sales*, *e-book*, and *free* entice readers to take (that is, open) what the sender is giving. Somewhat surprisingly, the list also includes a number of superlative modifiers such as *awesome*, *helpful*, and *great*. Although I generally advise caution when using these kinds of words in modern marketing, these data tell us that it may not hurt to experiment with them in e-mail subject lines. But don't forget the word *great* is just the sizzle; it's the offer that's the steak. Don't forget to include a meaty gift for your readers.

On the other side of the coin, we find words that are correlated with e-mails receiving lower-than-average CTRs (Figure 8.9). Many of these words, such as *evaluation*, *administration*, *consultation*, and *implementing*, are exceedingly boring and reek of jargon. Notice that the word *free* was on the most clicked words list, whereas the patrician *complimentary* was on the least clicked words list. Don't forget that your e-mails are being read on mobile phones while real life is being lived, and they're appearing in inboxes alongside cookout invitations from family and friends.

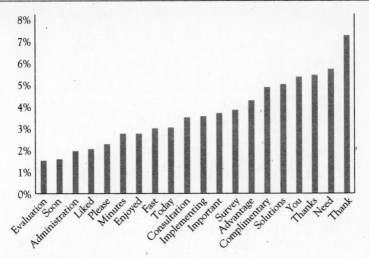

Figure 8.9   Least Clicked Lead Nurturing Subject Line Words

To get a broader sense of the ideal tone of e-mail subject lines, I used a linguistic lexicon developed by researcher Finn Nielsen called AFINN. The lexicon allowed me to tag words in subject lines with values for the strength of their positive or negative sentiment. A subject line's score is then calculated as the sum of the score of each constituent word. Large positive numbers indicate very positive sentiments, and large negative numbers indicate very negative sentiments. Small numbers indicate neutral tones.

I found that e-mails on either side of the sentiment scale, that is, those subject lines that were either very positive or very negative, had higher CTRs than those that were in the middle, neutral area (Figure 8.10). Passionate e-mails got clicked on more often. As we saw with the least clicked words list, boring e-mails don't get responses. When writing e-mail subject lines, be afraid of being neutral.

A common subject line pattern for some marketers and e-mail lists is to begin an e-mail with a parenthetical or bracketed word or phrase: often the name of the list, the newsletter, the company, or the type of offer contained in the e-mail. The idea is to tag the e-mail with something that will make each e-mail subject line recognizable even if the rest of the subject line changes for each message.

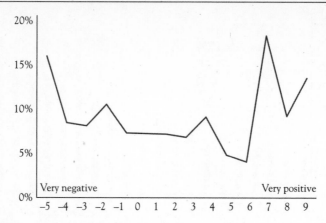

Figure 8.10   CTR by Subject Line Sentiment

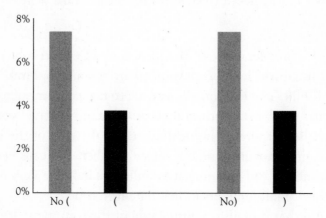

Figure 8.11   CTR by Use of Parentheses

When I analyzed the occurrence of parenthesis in subject lines, however, I found that e-mails with them performed significantly worse than e-mails without them (Figure 8.11). Parentheses aren't the right symbol for this use. In digital-native speak, parentheses function the same way they do regular text, for sidebar-type content that can be removed without destroying the overall meaning.

Squared brackets, on the other hand, have found a use online as a way to set apart text that functions as a tag. And I found that e-mails that used this type of bracketing did not have significantly lower response rates than e-mails that did not (Figure 8.12).

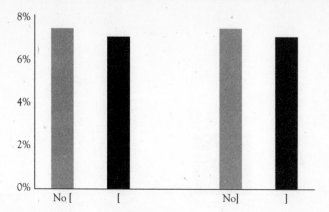

Figure 8.12   CTR by Use of Brackets

There is a subtle difference between the rounded and squared symbols, but incorrect usage can lead to an e-mail subject line having an unsettling awkwardness about them. If you decide to add a tag to your subject lines to promote memorability, use the right format.

My e-mail inbox is all about me. The most important e-mails I get (and the only ones I read regularly) are sent and written directly to me. Bulk e-mail is really the only exception to that rule. I get tons of e-mail every week written to huge lists of subscribers, and my interest in those e-mails is markedly lower. If I'm expecting that they'll have something in them that I really want, I'll read them, but I'd much rather be reading something that was meant just for me.

Personalization is the classic and still effective solution to this problem for e-mail marketers. The thinking goes that if you include your readers' names in the e-mail, especially in the subject line, they'll be more likely to open and read that e-mail. And my data analysis supports this. Those e-mails that included the receivers' first name had a higher CTR than those e-mails that did not include the first name (Figure 8.13).

Many e-mail readers are savvy to this tactic these days, but it still works. Don't pretend you're the cleverest sender of e-mail ever; your readers will know that you've included their name through an automated database system. Don't try to fool them. But do personalize. When they're filtering through their inboxes, their name will

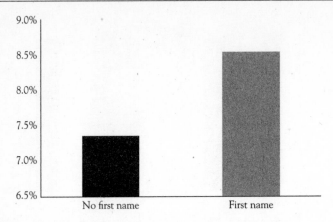

Figure 8.13   CTR by First Name Personalization

grab their attention, even if only momentarily, and give your e-mail that precious split second of awareness you need.

Most e-mail marketing service provider systems allow you to send both HTML and plain text e-mails to your subscribers, typically based on their preferences. I've never been a big fan of asking readers to specify the format of e-mails they prefer to receive because I like to keep my sign-up forms as short as possible. But on the surface, it would seem like this isn't a horrible idea, asking people what they want you to send them.

In one of my surveys, I asked takers what format they want to receive e-mails in and I was surprised by the answer. Only 12 percent said they want to get plain text e-mails (Figure 8.14). Users are mostly using e-mail reading clients, both on their desktop environments and mobile devices, that correctly render HTML, so they like getting messages in that format.

For marketers this means that you should feel pretty safe removing the format preference question from your forms, especially if you test this change and can determine it increases your form completion rate. Send in HTML, and the vast majority of your readers will be happy.

Along the lines of the HTML versus plain text question, I've also asked e-mail users if they prefer getting e-mails from companies

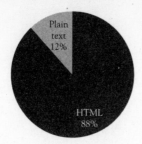

Figure 8.14   In What Format Do You Prefer to Receive E-Mail Messages from Companies?

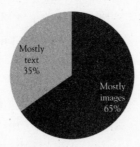

Figure 8.15   Do You Prefer That E-Mails from Companies Contain Mostly Images or Mostly Text?

that are composed of mostly text or imagery. This was an even more surprising result: 65 percent of respondents told me they like getting image-heavy e-mails (Figure 8.15).

My wife told me she had read my survey and felt the same way as most of the takers, so I asked her to explain. She signs up for e-mails to get stuff (like most subscribers), and she wants senders just to send a picture of what they're offering and a link to a place to get it—quick and simple delivery of the value offer.

For marketers, the takeaway is simple: experiment with sending e-mails with big images. Take an enticing photo of your product or whip up a visual representation of your content, make it clickable, and send it to your list. Watch your response rates and learn.

Before I did my research, I used to write e-mails and focus on having one strong call to action and one really obvious link for

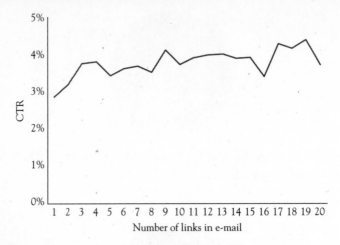

Figure 8.16   Effect of Number of Links on CTR

readers to click on. I figured less was more and the fewer distractions I offered my subscribers, the higher my response rates would be. Data have a way of messing up assumptions like these.

In the huge MailChimp data set, I found that there is a positive correlation between the CTR percentage of an e-mail and the number of links in it. The more links in an e-mail, the more clicks that e-mail will drive to your site (Figure 8.16). Now when I send e-mails, I put in as many links as I reasonably can: big links, little links, image links, and text links.

Having a lot of links also indicates that you're filling your e-mails with useful content, a good habit to get into. Since your subscribers want to know what's in it for them, the more you're offering them, the better your e-mails will perform.

Along the same lines as my last point about stuffing your e-mails to the brim with value for your subscribers, I found that e-mails that have an ampersand in the subject line tend to have higher CTRs than e-mails that do not (Figure 8.17). At first this data point might seem a little confusing, but if we think about it for a moment, the reason becomes clear.

Don't take this to mean that if you take your existing subject line and slap on an ampersand that you're instantly going to get

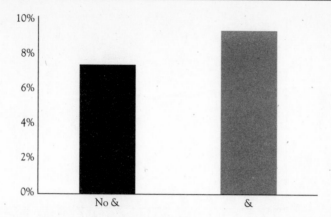

Figure 8.17   CTR by Use of Ampersand

more clicks. That's not what I'm saying. Instead, imagine the kind of e-mail marketing behavior that results in ampersands being used and duplicate that.

If you're using ampersands, it's likely you're trying to communicate a lot of value in your subject line. So much value, in fact, you're running out of space and can't spare three characters for the word *and*, so you have to abbreviate with an ampersand. You're giving your subscribers lots of value and, naturally, lots of stuff to click on.

And if more clicks weren't enough to entice you to stuff your e-mails full of links, take a look at the relationship between the number of links in an e-mail and unsubscription rates. E-mails with more links tend to have fewer people unsubscribing (Figure 8.18).

Again, I don't think the reason here is because of a direct relationship between the number of href tags in an e-mail and unsubscription behavior; instead, think about what lots of links in an e-mail means. It means the e-mail is offering readers lots of things to buy, read, download, and enjoy. E-mails with lots of links are providing lots of value. Readers who get value out of your e-mails are less likely to unsubscribe.

I also found that longer subject lines tend to have higher CTRs (Figure 8.19). A long subject line is another indicator of a meaty e-mail. As a reader is scanning through his or her inbox, deciding whether or not to open each e-mail with only a moment's glance,

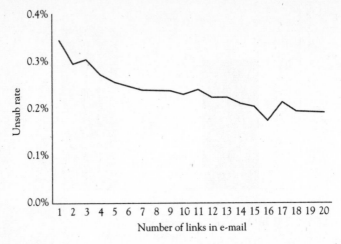

Figure 8.18   Effect of Number of Links on Unsubscribe Rate

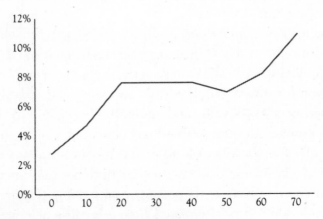

Figure 8.19   CTR by Subject Line Length

a lengthy subject line promising a ton of value will catch his or her attention. Long subject lines take full advantage of all of the potential real estate offered to e-mail senders. Use as much of the space you're given by e-mail clients to convince your readers to open and click on your e-mails.

When you're writing subject lines, don't add more unnecessary words or characters to make them longer. If you're finding that your subject lines are too short, it's a problem with the content of the

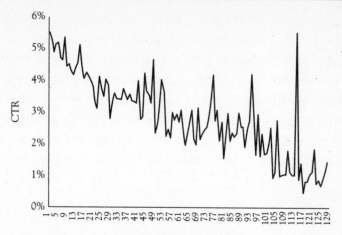

Days since subscription

Figure 8.20   Effect of Subscriber Recency on CTR

e-mail, not the wording of the subject. Add more valuable content to the e-mail, and the length of the subject line will naturally increase.

In all of my analysis of e-mail marketing and response rates, the most significant factor I found was the recency or "age" of the subscriber to an e-mail list (Figure 8.20). That is, the more recently someone signed up to your e-mail list, the more likely that person is to open, read, and click on your e-mails.

This is a problem for marketers who send only regular e-mail newsletters; they're not optimizing for subscriber recency. The easiest way to take advantage of this phenomenon is transactional e-mail and lead nurturing–style campaigns. Each action on your site where a visitor gives you his or her e-mail address—be it a subscription, e-book download, or purchase—should trigger a set of e-mails to that person. Strike while the iron is hot. Send an e-mail or two as soon as you can after someone signs up.

When I analyzed lead nurturing–style e-mail campaigns, I found reinforcement about my last point on recency. Lead nurturing campaigns are generally drip marketing chains of e-mails that are each sent a specified number of days after a user takes an action on a site. Common patterns are to send e-mails on the first, third, fifth, and tenth days.

The data show that the longer an e-mail is separate from the user's action, the lower the response rate of that e-mail. The first few days have great CTRs, but after that, it's all downhill (Figure 8.21). E-mail your newest subscribers; they're your best audience.

Figure 8.22 represents perhaps my most surprising finding on e-mail marketing. In many organizations there is a struggle between the desire to send more e-mail and the fear of burning out an e-mail list with too many sends. When I analyzed the huge data set from MailChimp and looked at unsubscriptions and the average number of sends per month to an e-mail list, I found that unsubscriptions

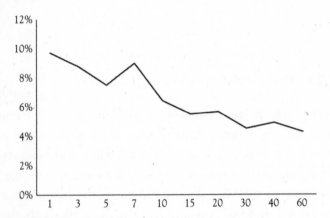

Figure 8.21   CTR by Days after the Start of a Lead Nurturing Campaign

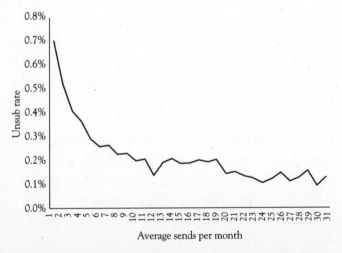

Figure 8.22   Effect of Sending Frequency on Unsubscribe Rate

are the highest for lists that receive very little e-mail. In fact, as the number of sends per month increased—up to one e-mail every day—the unsubscription rate decreased. Frequently e-mailed subscribers unsubscribe less.

This is likely because the users on high-volume lists have come to expect a lot of e-mail from those lists and are genuinely interested in what the list owners are sending them. If they weren't getting anything of value, they would have already opted out.

Marketers should not be afraid to experiment with frequent e-mail sends. These data are based on an aggregate, generalized data set, so your list may be different. But this should remove the fear of testing a more intense e-mail schedule.

The other side of the frequency coin is, of course, the CTR of those lists that are sent a ton of e-mail very frequently. I found that CTRs were highest for lists that received only one or two e-mails per month, but beyond that, there was no big decline in performance of lists that were e-mailed between 3 and 30 times a month (Figure 8.23).

If you're getting a certain CTR with your current frequency and you can double that frequency without halving your CTR, the net

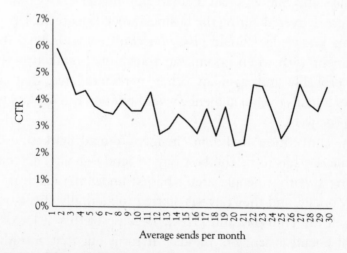

Figure 8.23   Effect of Sending Frequency on CTR

effect on your net clicks sent from e-mails will be positive. Sending more e-mail is not the marketing taboo many of us had previously thought it to be. As long as you're following the guidelines set forth in the rest of this chapter and sending targeted, personalized, and value-packed e-mails, sending more of them is better.

Increasing your frequency also gives you more freedom to test the other suggestions I've laid out for you in this chapter, especially timing. And a faster e-mail schedule will allow you to e-mail your most recent subscribers a few more times than you'd be able to otherwise.

Timing data for any kind of online marketing is always tricky. Best practice data is always generalized based on large data sets that may vary from the behavior of your specific audience. And there are time zone considerations to take into account. The best way to use timing data like this is as a blueprint for experimentation. If one of my data points suggests a different time or day than you're currently sending, test it and see if it works for you.

During the business week, I get hundreds of e-mails every day. I don't read most of it. I simply don't have the time or the attention span for them. On the weekends, however, I get much less e-mail, and consequently, I read a lot more of it. The data seem to bear this out across billions of sends. Those messages that were delivered on Saturdays and Sundays had dramatically higher CTRs than those that were delivered during the business week (Figure 8.24).

This knowledge should give you two new additional days to experiment with when optimizing your e-mail marketing timing. You'll probably find, as many other marketers have, that certain kinds of e-mails to your audience work better on the weekends than during the week.

It's "conventional wisdom" in many e-mail marketing circles that Tuesday has to be the best day to send e-mail. The common thinking says that people aren't buried under the catch-up work from Monday, and they haven't started to mentally check out like they will on Thursday and Friday. Because of this, a lot of commercial e-mail is sent on Tuesday. It turns out that according to

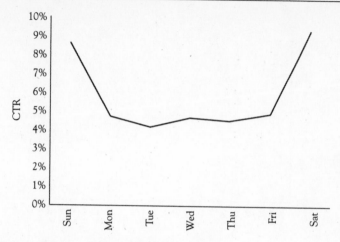

Figure 8.24   Effect of Day of Week on CTR

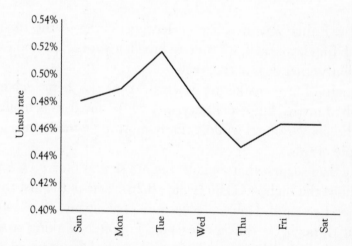

Figure 8.25   Effect of Day of Week on Unsubscribe Rate

the data, unsubscription rates are the highest on Tuesday, probably because of this very fact (Figure 8.25).

Readers may have gotten one too many boring, bulk marketing messages clogging their inbox that morning, and they finally started pulling the unsubscribe trigger and your e-mails got caught in the cross fire. Or maybe it's hard to tell your carefully crafted and relevant e-mails apart from the less worthwhile spam sent on

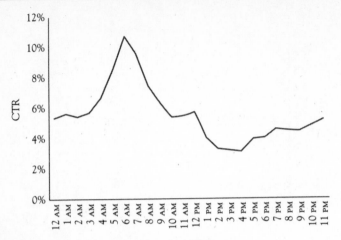

Figure 8.26　Effect of Time of Day on CTR

Tuesday. Either way, if you're currently sticking to the timeworn love of Tuesday e-mail, it's time to broaden your scope and experiment with other days of the week.

Much of my marketing scientist time is spent debunking cherished myths, but every once in a while, my data actually support the conventional wisdom. Early-morning e-mail sends are an example of this.

My data suggest that e-mails that are sent at 6 or 7 AM Eastern time have the highest CTRs (Figure 8.26). One of the first things I do when I get up and into my office is to open up my inbox and start wading through. As the day wears on, I'm often working on something with my head down and it's much more difficult for an e-mail to steal my attention away. If your e-mails are there, first thing in the morning when I'm drinking my coffee and reading my e-mail, you've got a much better chance that I'll read and click on them.

9

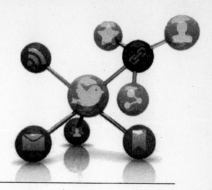

Lead Generation

I'VE SPENT THE past four years working at a business-to-business (B2B) software company. Our marketing team's bottom line is the number of leads and subsequently sales we drive. Naturally, one of the largest chunks of research I've done is into the science of lead generation—how to get more people to fill out more lead forms. If you're a B2B marketer reading this chapter, awesome; I've got some data that I hope will make your job easier.

But, if you're not focused on lead generation, perhaps you work for an e-commerce site or a subscription-based magazine; this chapter will still have some useful jewels for you. We all want more e-mail subscribers, and an e-mail subscription form is essentially a very short lead form. This chapter will help you convert more viewers into subscribers. You'll also read data about optimizing buttons (like your checkout button) to make them more clickable.

I know the phrase *lead generation* can make some eyes gloss over, but stick with this chapter for a while and I think you'll be surprised.

At HubSpot, many of our customers are focused on lead generation, which means that I get access to all sorts of data about lead generation that is nearly impossible to get from any other source. When I started digging into the mountains of information, the first thing I looked at was the performance, based on visit-to-lead conversion rates, of traffic coming from various sources to our customers' websites.

At first, the data in Figure 9.1 isn't that surprising. Paid traffic converts at the highest percentage. It makes sense that it would; after all, if you're paying for it, you're picking the traffic carefully

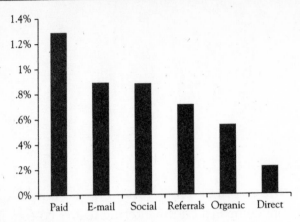

Figure 9.1　Conversion Rate by Traffic Score

and planning the pages it lands on with a precision not seen in most other channels.

What is surprising, however, is the next two bars on the graph. E-mail and social media traffic convert, for thousands of our customers, at equally high rates. Most online marketers recognize that e-mail traffic is a valuable and laser-targeted channel, but many hold a misconception that direct response lead generation is difficult, if not impossible, to do on social media. My data suggest that idea is a myth.

A core concept of inbound marketing is the practice of enticing potential customers with valuable content-based offers. To better understand how people think about these offers, I did a survey in which I asked respondents to rank seven different types of content by how valuable they believe them to be.

The top six offers all performed similarly, with the comprehensive-sounding *downloadable kit* ranked the highest and the somewhat boring-sounding *white paper* ranked second lowest. The one standout (in a bad way) offer, *demo/consultation*, was the only type listed that plainly indicated the beginning of a sales process rather than an educational, informational, or useful offer (Figure 9.2).

When you're trying to draw people into your brand like a magnet and trade them something of value for their contact information,

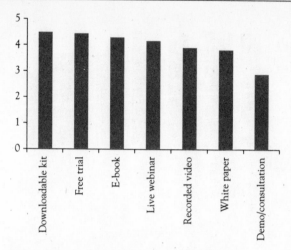

Figure 9.2   Offer Types Ranked by Perceived Value

you should do so with something your potential customers believe is valuable. Don't rely on contact forms or demo request forms to drive all of your lead generation. Your visitors know those kinds of offers mean someone is going to call them up and try to sell them something. Save those offers for your hot leads who've already downloaded your other content offers.

One benefit of doing surveys is that I can ask survey takers information about themselves that is often hard to get through other means. In the offer-type survey, I asked respondents for their gender and broke down their perceived value rankings into male and female groups.

I found that while, for the most part, both men and women ranked the offers similarly, there was one pattern of difference. Women reported finding offers types such as *free trial* and *live webinar* more valuable, whereas men preferred *e-book, recorded video,* and *white paper* (Figure 9.3). Women seemed to prefer the real-time experiential offers, whereas my male respondents preferred offers that they could download and consume at their leisure.

The key here for marketers is to know your audience. Know if they skew male or female and know what kinds of content they want. My data are based on huge data sets, and your specific audience

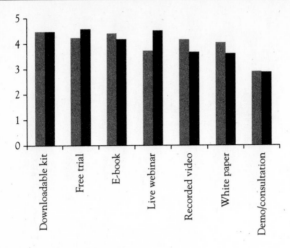

Figure 9.3 Perceived Offer Value by Gender

may differ. Don't be afraid to conduct your own surveys with your own audience.

Going back to our customer data set, I began looking at the conversion rate (visit-to-lead) of tens of thousands of landing pages. I first noticed that landing pages using certain words had higher conversion rates than landing pages that did not mention those words.

Words that indicate the landing page is offering a valuable content type, such as *webinar, white paper, download, chapter, tools,* and *report,* correlated with landing pages having higher conversion rates than landing pages that did not use those words. In Figure 9.4, you can see the performance of the landing pages using these words in the light-colored bars compared with those that did not in the dark-colored bars.

As noticed in the survey data, people prefer content that will teach them to do something or tools that can make their lives easier or their work more successful. To take advantage of this preference, marketers need to clearly communicate the kind of value they're offering on their landing pages.

Of all the common landing page words I studied, one stuck out as constantly associated with landing pages having higher-than-average conversion rates: *free* (Figure 9.5).

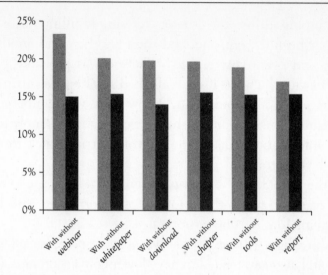

Figure 9.4 Conversion Rate by Reference to Content Type

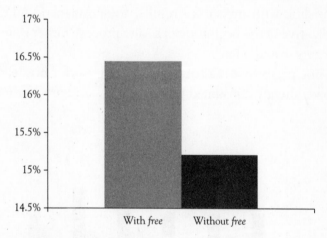

Figure 9.5 Conversion Rate by Occurrence of *Free*

Because inbound lead generation is essentially an exchange of value from the company for the user's contact information, it is important to visitors that the value they get be free of charge. *Free* is one of the most powerful words in the marketer's tool kit, but it must be used with caution. In my focus groups, a common concern raised was that sometimes some offers seem "too good to be true." One focus group participant told me a story of being lured by an ad that promised free UGG boots for simply filling out a couple of forms. She filled out one, and then another, and another and another, and eventually realized that she was probably going to have to pay for the boots if she really had any hope of getting them.

Users are not stupid. They know that you're not going to offer them expensive boots or high-priced gadgets simply for their contact information. Take care to avoid getting stuck in the too good to be true trap.

On the flip side of the high-performing landing page words coin are the common words that I found to be correlated with landing pages having lowered conversion rates.

Landing pages that used words such as *quote, price, request, services, contact,* and *questions* tended to have lower conversion rates (as seen in the light-colored bars in Figure 9.6) than landing pages that did not use those words (as seen in the dark-colored bars in Figure 9.6). Again, in line with my survey results, these low-performing words were indicative of the beginning of a sales process, rather than a valuable, content-based offer.

Landing pages that use these words are great for hot leads, people who've already consumed content offers and are ready to start

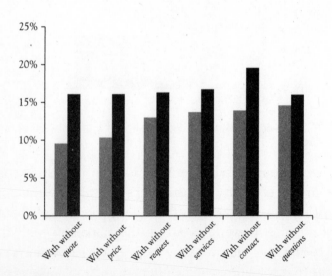

Figure 9.6   Conversion Rate by Reference to Contact

buying what you're selling. But don't rely on them to generate a ton of inbound leads, as they're not as enticing as e-book- or webinar-type offers.

Similar to the performance of the word *free*, contests and sweepstakes are perennial lead generation favorites. Companies can offer large prizes without incurring huge costs and visitors aren't too bothered by too good to be true concerns.

In my data set, I found that landing pages that used the word *contest* or the word *winner* tended to have higher visit-to-lead conversion rates than landing pages that did not use those words (Figure 9.7).

I did several focus groups where I asked people about landing pages. I didn't use that phrase, but rather described pages that asked for information about them in exchange for something. A topic that came up often was contests and sweepstakes. My focus group participants were often asked for their information in exchange for a chance to win a prize. They knew the difference between contests and sweepstakes, although they didn't always know which word was which. (For the record, a contest requires entrants to do or make something, whereas a sweepstakes simply requires entry and a random selection.) Participants reported entering both types but had different expectations. They would put more time into a contest, as

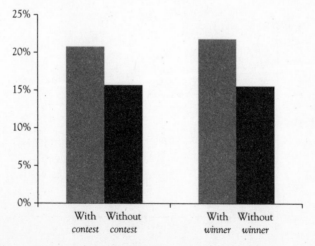

Figure 9.7   Conversion Rate by Reference to a Contest

they believed they had some control over their chances of winning. Be aware of which you're planning to use and tailor the amount of effort required to enter (low effort for sweepstakes, higher for contests).

One of the most common pieces of lead generation advice is to reduce the number of questions you're asking visitors to your landing pages, and this makes a lot of sense. In fact, when I first got to HubSpot and saw our large form, that was the first thing I thought of: I wanted to shrink them. But every time we've tested removing one or more fields, we've never seen any huge increase in conversion rate.

And when I looked at our customer data, I found a similar result. As the number of form fields on the landing pages increased, there was no major decline in visit-to-lead conversion rates (Figure 9.8).

When you're offering your visitors valuable content, they tend to be willing to invest a little bit of time into filling out your forms. And my focus group work uncovered a key variable in that equation: Can visitors get what you're offering somewhere else? If you're trying to entice them with something they can find more easily with a quick Google search, your big form probably won't work. But if you're the only good source of what they want, you'll get a

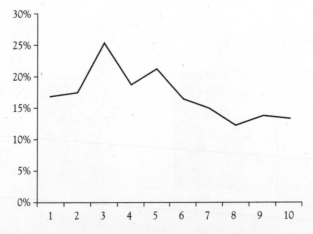

Figure 9.8   Conversion Rate by Number of Form Fields

little more slack. Offer something good and don't worry about a big form.

I dug into the form field data a bit further and looked at three different types of fields separately. The first one I investigated was the simple text field. This is the most common field on the Web. It's one line and is used for information like first name, company name, and street address.

I found that as the number of simple text input fields increased, there was no dramatic drop off in conversion rates—at least until there were 15 on a single page, which is kind of a lot (Figure 9.9).

The next form field type I analyzed was the select box. These are the multiple-choice drop-down boxes that are often used for information such as state; they are less common than text fields, but not very rare.

In contrast to simple text fields, I found that as the number of select boxes on a landing page increased from one to five, there was a significant decline in the conversion rate of those landing pages (Figure 9.10). Drop-down boxes often mean that the landing page is asking more complex or detailed information, and a long list of them can be more intimidating. Use these with more caution on your pages.

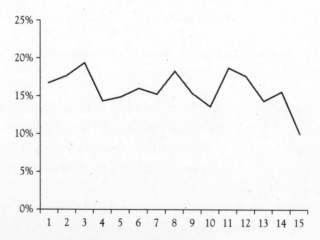

Figure 9.9 Conversion Rate by Text Fields

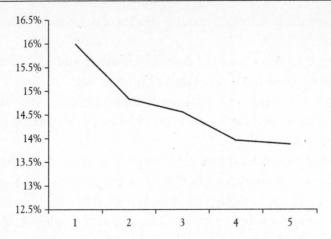

Figure 9.10   Conversion Rate by Number of Selected Boxes

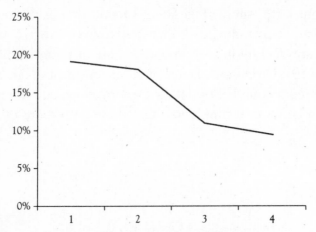

Figure 9.11   Conversion Rate by Number of Textareas

Last, I investigated the textarea field type. These are the ulti-mate buzzkill of input types. They're the big, rectangular, multiline, paragraph entry fields. Whenever I see one of these, I groan a little inside, because it makes me feel like I'm expected to write a college admissions essay.

And, somewhat expectedly, I found that as the number of tex-tareas on a landing page climbed from one to four, the conversion rate of those pages was halved (Figure 9.11). Clearly, it's difficult to

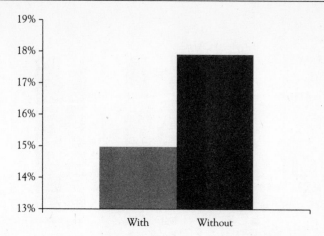

Figure 9.12   Conversion Rate by Occurrence of the Word *Age*

convince visitors to spend the time required to write four essays just to get your free e-book. If you find yourself adding one of them to landing page, first ask if it's really necessary; if it is, try to avoid using very many of them.

Going beyond just form field types, I analyzed certain kinds of information requests on landing pages. One common type I found that correlated with diminished landing page performance was age. Landing pages that asked for the visitor's age (the light-colored bar in Figure 9.12) had lower conversion rates than landing pages that did not (the dark-colored bar in Figure 9.12).

In my focus groups I asked participants about specific types of questions on landing pages, and the general consensus was that they were okay with providing only information that made sense. If you're offering a downloadable e-book, do you really need users' phone numbers? Maybe if you're offering a webinar you do, but in that case, you don't need their street address, do you? Be sure the information you're requesting either has an obvious reason or explain your need and planned use of it. For most marketing offers, asking someone's age is a strange and somewhat intrusive question—unless you're offering free beer.

I also looked at different kinds of physical address questions. I found that landing pages that asked for information such as street,

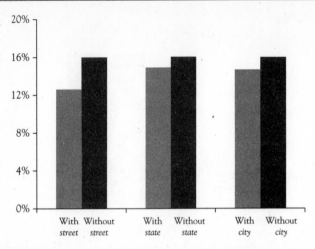

Figure 9.13   Conversion Rate by Occurrence of Address

state, or city had lower conversion rates than landing pages that did not ask for that information (Figure 9.13).

But there is an interesting pattern if we compare the size of the effects these words have on landing page performance. Asking for zip code–level information—which my focus group participants did not report having a problem providing—had a much smaller negative effect than did asking for street-level information.

People in my focus groups assumed that businesses had access to zip code–level (city and state) information about them anyway, so they didn't hesitate to provide it. But when a company starts asking for street-level information, they begin to worry that someone is going to show up at their house around dinnertime and try to sell something or that they're going to start getting a ton of junk mail.

If you really need to ask for the street address of your leads tell them why you need it and what you're going to do with it.

Similar to street address, I found that landing pages that used words such as *phone* and *call* had lower conversion rates than pages that did not (Figure 9.14). These words indicate that you're asking

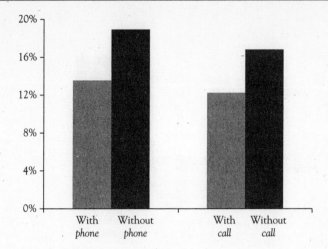

Figure 9.14   Conversion Rate by Reference to *Telephone*

for their phone number and that you intend to use it to call your leads and have your salespeople hassle them.

Again, if you need to ask for a visitor's phone number, clearly explain, on the landing page, why you need it and what you plan to do with it. But don't be surprised if it lowers your conversion rate and be prepared to experiment with using forms without that question.

Let's do a little experiment. I'm going to say (or type, as is the case) a word, and I want you to tell me the first word that comes to your mind. Ready? Okay here goes: *submit*.

I've done that test with audiences both virtual and physical, all over the world; although the specific responses vary, they're typically not positive.

Submit is the default text used on form submission buttons at the end of Web forms, and I found that landing pages that use buttons with that word tend to have lower conversion rates than landing pages that do not use that word (Figure 9.15).

Typically, you'll want to use a word that more specifically identifies the actual action the user is doing. If you're offering users a

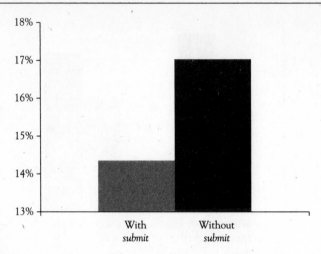

Figure 9.15   Conversion Rate by Occurrence of *Submit*

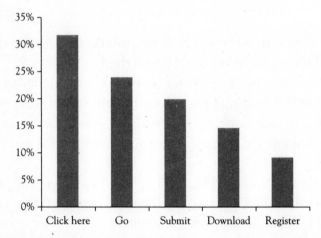

Figure 9.16   Clicks by Button Text

downloadable e-book, the correct word is *download*. If they're sign-ing up for a webinar, *register* is appropriate.

If you can't be bothered to use a specific word on your submit buttons, I did a little test to find better default wording. I made a page that contained five buttons, each with different text on them: *click here, go, submit, download,* and *register*. I then asked 500 people, without context, to click one button. Each visitor to the page saw the buttons in a randomly shuffled order and could only click a button once.

Click here and *go* performed the best, being low-commitment, high-action words. *Download* and *register* were clicked the least because they indicated that something might happen after the user clicked them, and without any context that sounded like a lot of hassle (Figure 9.16).

So again, use a specific word where you can, but at least use a better default than *submit*.

PART

IV

Analytics

10

Analytics

Most of this book has been about data collected from a wide variety of industries, but ultimately the best data you can use to direct your marketing efforts will be your own. Your audience may be different from the average. This is where analytics comes in. This is where you'll need to start doing your own science.

This chapter will start with four pieces of data I gathered from a survey I conducted with marketers. I wanted to gain a qualitative understanding of how marketers are using analytics data. You should use these graphs as a way to benchmark your current performance. Are you ahead of the curve or behind?

After that, I'll introduce you to the scientific method as it can be applied to your own website and marketing efforts. You'll learn four continual steps you should be doing to become a scientifically driven marketer.

The first question I asked in my survey to marketers about analytics was, "Do you pay for analytics?" I'm personally of the opinion that there are great tools both paid (the company I work for, HubSpot, comes to mind) and free (Google Analytics is the market leader in free analytics systems) that marketers can use to get insights into their metrics. This survey, as with most that I do, was designed to build a qualitative picture of the problem I'm attempting to solve.

I found that a full 76 percent of the hundreds of marketers who answered my survey reported that they do not pay for analytics software (Figure 10.1). This is not to say that they're using free software;

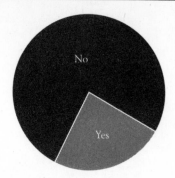

Figure 10.1 Do You Pay for Analytics?

it could also mean that they're not using any analytics software. The latter thought is much scarier than the former.

I often say in presentations, "Marketing without data is like driving with your eyes closed." If my survey had asked, "Do you pay for a windshield on your car?" what do you think the answers would have been?

Next, I asked, "How often do analytics factor into your decisions?" Here at HubSpot, we're obsessed with metrics and hard data. We analyze every square centimeter of our business, both on the marketing team and throughout the rest of the organization. And I'm personally a very analytical marketer, so I asked this question to understand how much the rest of the industry was relying on analytics to drive their marketing efforts.

Although I would have liked to see the "always" bar as the tallest, I'm relatively pleased to see that the most common answer was "frequently" (Figure 10.2). But between "sometimes," "rarely," and "never," roughly 45 percent of the marketers who took my survey are not being driven by analytics as much as they should be. Forty-five percent are opening their eyes sometimes or rarely when they're hurtling down the highway.

Then I posed the most contentious possible survey question in the field of marketing analytics to my survey takers. I asked if they measure the return on investment (ROI) of four major channels in online marketing: social media, SEO, paid, and e-mail. They

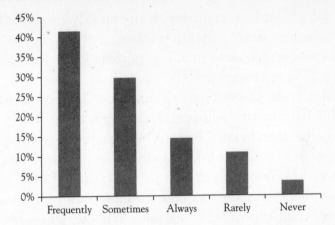

Figure 10.2   How Often Do Analytics Factor into Your Decisions?

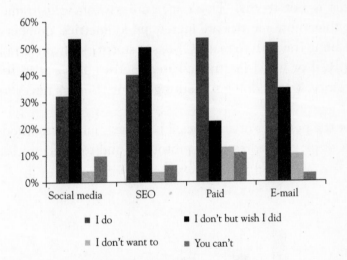

Figure 10.3   Do You Measure the ROI of These?

chose answers from four possible options: "I do," "I don't, but wish I did," "I don't want to" (it felt weird even typing this one into the SurveyMonkey), and "You can't."

As, I expected, the "I do" answers were highest for paid and e-mail channels, followed by SEO (Figure 10.3). Unfortunately, social media was the channel with the fewest ROI-measuring marketers, with just over 30 percent answering "I do." Somewhat reassuringly, the highest answer for the social channel was "I don't, but wish I did." I can be consoled with the knowledge that although many marketers aren't currently measuring the dollars-and-cents ROI of social media, more than half of them know you can, know they should be, and want to be.

Finally, I asked survey respondents what they considered their most important metric. Although I was happy to see that "visitors" ranked higher than "visits," I was rather unhappy to see that "leads" and "sales" were ranked third and fourth, respectively (Figure 10.4). If you take only one thing away from this chapter, I hope it is that the most important metric for your business to be measuring is the one most closely connected to real sales. Website visitors aren't paying your payroll or keeping the lights on; customers are.

This is not to say, "Don't measure visitors/visits/traffic," but rather that those metrics are merely proxy metrics, numbers to be found along the path to real ROI-based statistics. If you're not measuring ROI or you'd list traffic-based metrics above it in terms of importance, you're doing something wrong. But it's never too late to fix that.

For the purposes of analytics, I boil the scientific method down to four steps: define, research, prototype, and test (Figure 10.5). In

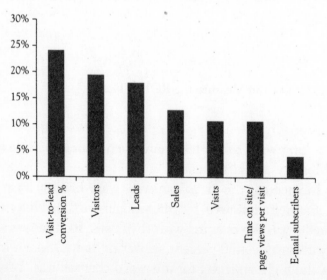

Figure 10.4   What Is Your Most Important Metric?

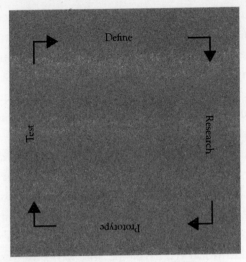

Figure 10.5   The Scientific Method for Analytics

the define stage, you're asking (and answering) the question, "What do I want to improve?" At the research step, the question is, "What does my audience want?" While prototyping, ask, "What will I test?" And finally, when testing, the goal is to answer, "Which variation performed the best?"

When I present the scientific method to marketers, I do so through a graphic like the one shown in Figure 10.5. We should not look at the method as simply a set of steps to be completed once and then discarded. They're a continual process through which all of your analytics and metric-driven enhancements will be made.

Define

The key to getting useful answers in any endeavor, and especially in marketing, is asking the correct questions. The place to begin your analytics work is to ask yourself, "What do I want (or better yet, need) to improve?" You're trying here to identify what will be your key performance indicators (KPIs). You may even already know them.

Typically, the first few times you use this process, the best answers to that question will be metrics very close to your dollars-and-cents

ROI actions. If you're a lead generation–based business, you'll want to get more leads, which can be accomplished by increasing the visit-to-lead conversion rate of your landing pages. E-commerce companies will be aiming at actual on-site sales and looking to reduce shopping cart abandonment and increase checkout completion.

After you've focused on the conversion rates and metrics closest to your money-making actions, you'll want to move up the funnel and start working on those metrics I call proxy, or canary-in-the-coal-mine, metrics. These are the actions that typically lead to a sale. E-mail subscriptions are a great example of this. E-mail marketing tends to have a higher conversion rate than other channels, so if you can convert a nonsubscribed visitor to a subscriber, you'll increase the likelihood that that person will buy from you. Social media metrics can be slightly more abstract but still useful examples: retweets lead to increased traffic. More traffic means more conversions.

An interesting subset of these proxy metrics that I find useful are on-site engagement metrics. Increased pages per visit and time on site are clear indicators of a highly engaged visitor and generally one who is more likely to convert into a lead or sale. After you've exhausted your direct ROI metrics and close proxies, experiment with improving these engagement metrics for some of your biggest traffic sources.

Research

The next step is the research phase. Here you'll be gathering as much information as you possibly can to answer the question, "What does my audience want?" It can be tempting, and often even successful, to simply assume that you are very similar to or understanding of your target audience and can therefore just guess at what they want. If you spend a few minutes talking to the people in your company who interact with customers and potential customers—often salespeople and support folks—you'll quickly hear a few of their top wants and needs. These are great places to start.

To go further than these anecdotal sources is as simple as doing a survey. There are a ton of tools available on the Web for conducting easy surveys, from the free Google Spreadsheet forms to the inexpensive SurveyMonkey. I've used both for my research and can recommend them. An entire book could be written (and many have) on how to design surveys, but the simplest question to ask is "What is your biggest _____ challenge?" The blank space would be the topical area your company sells solutions for. At HubSpot, we sell marketing software, so we ask, "What is your biggest marketing challenge?"

Focus groups are another easy way to perform qualitative research. Contact a few existing customers or potential customers and offer them a small reward (Amazon gift cards work well) to come into your office and talk for an hour. Get their permission to record the session and set up an unobtrusive camera in the room. Again, many books have been written about how to best perform focus groups, so pick one of those up if you're interested, but don't be intimidated by the idea; they're a lot easier and more rewarding than you'd expect.

The social Web can also provide a sort of on-demand focus group if you know where to look. Go to Twitter search and type in a word that describes what your company sells, then a space, and then a question mark. You'll get results composed not only of people talking about your niche, but people asking questions about your niche. They're telling you exactly what they want and need to know.

Your analytics software also provides a treasure trove of data about your audience, the most valuable of which is the list of search engine keywords that are sending traffic to your site. Look over the list, start at the top, the most popular terms, but also dig way into the long tail and find those really specific terms a few people a month are using. Does your website have content about those queries?

Also look at the conversion rates of traffic coming from those keywords, and look at the time on site of visitors who found your site using them. If the word is relevant to your business but the traffic is performing poorly, those words are what your audience needs.

Prototype

Once you know what you want to improve and you have an idea of what your audience wants from you, you can begin to design ways to deliver improved experiences to them and increased metrics to yourself. In the prototyping stage, you'll be asking the question, "What will I test?"

The majority of this book is full of best practice suggestions for nearly every aspect of your online marketing efforts. These data were collected from huge data sets. When you read a piece of advice like that, apply it in the prototyping stage and test it. Are your e-mails not performing as well as you'd like them to? Crack open the e-mail chapter and test some ideas from there. Is your Facebook page languishing? Experiment with some suggestions from that chapter.

Typically, the easiest place for a marketer to begin designing tests is on a landing page, those pages on your site where visitors land and are first met with an opportunity to convert. Even if you're not in a lead generation business, the lead generation chapter is full of data you may find useful when you're trying to get more e-mail subscribers.

Test

The fourth—but not final, because it's a cycle, remember—stage in the process is the actual testing of the prototypes you designed in the previous step. You're essentially asking the question, "Which variation performs the best?"

Split testing is the easiest way to approach testing. Simply make a second, or third, variation of your landing page, e-mail, or call to action and split the traffic between the existing version and the prototype. Most marketing software can help you accomplish this, and even many content management systems can be cajoled into doing it.

An even simpler, but less rigorous, version is something called a time split. Simply replace the existing element with the new variation for a period of time and then compare the performance during the time the new version was up with the performance before that. Time splits can work in a jam, but differences in traffic between the two time periods can confuse results.

Multivariate testing is a more complex method of testing in which you are replacing and testing specific elements on a page, rather than the whole page. This can help a more advanced marketer test through a large number of possible changes very quickly to identify the best possible combination.

Index